FOR

LUXURIOUS TRAVEL

SUPERIOR SUN SALOON
S.M.T. COACHES ARE BEST

With Toilet accommodation and all the latest known improvements that enhance the joys of Motoring, these Coaches are the progressive step born of experience

We have always some new ideas for the comfort of passengers . . . . .

H.V. Burlingham Ltd.

MOTOR BODY BUILDERS

PRESTON NEW ROAD . . . . BLACKPOOL

Phone : MARTON, BLACKPOOL 251-252

BODYWORK BY
H·V·BURLINGHAM, LIMITED
BLACKPOOL.

£3.25

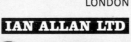

LONDON

IAN ALLAN LTD

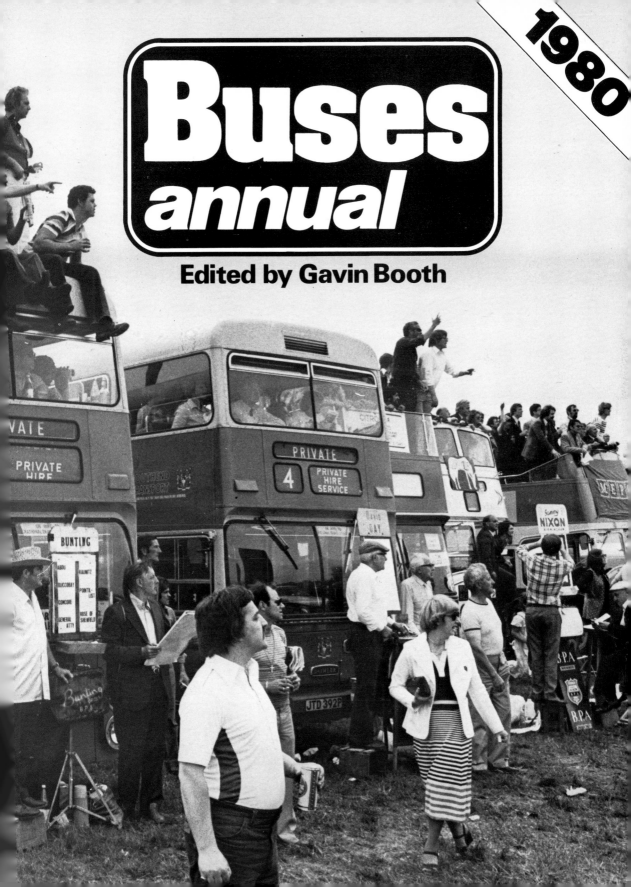

Buses
annual

Edited by Gavin Booth

1980

Acknowledgements

The photographs in *Buses Annual 1980* were supplied by:

John Aldridge 75-79, 91
Ian Allan Library 9 (upper), 81 (lower)
Dave Allerton 106
G. H. F. Atkins 7 (lower), 36-40, 89 (lower)
Gavin Booth Cover, 29, 61 (lower), 62 (foot), 84, 90, 92 (lower), 101 (upper), 104 (centre)
Gavin Booth Collection Front endpapers, 86 (lower), rear endpapers
Stewart J. Brown 25 (upper), 26 (upper), 27 (top), 62 (centre), 64-69, 81 (lower)
Stewart J. Brown Collection 88 (lower), 104 (top)
G. Coxon 82, 116-121
Michael Dryhurst 26 (lower), 48-56
Duple 63 (lower), 102
D. Fereday Glenn 22-24, 83 (lower)
Robert Grieves 92 (upper), 109, 111
W. J. Haynes 7 (upper)
Robert E. Jowitt 30-35
Charles F. Klapper 93-99
Leyland Vehicles 27 (centre)
R. C. Ludgate 41-46, 89 (upper)
MCW 103 (lower)
G. R. Mills 25 (lower), 87 (lower), 104 (foot), 105 (foot), 112-115
Alan Millar 125-129
T. W. Moore 1, 11-15, 47
Stewart MacDonald 122-124
A. Moyes 16-21, 27 (foot), 83 (upper)
Park Royal 105 (top, centre)
Martin J. Perry 57, 58
Greg Travers 107
Travel Press 5, 9 (lower), 10
Van Hool 63 (upper)
Vauxhall 59, 60, 61 (upper), 62 (top), 101 (lower)
Viewfinder 85, 86 (upper), 87 (upper), 88 (upper), 103 (upper)
John Ward 110
George F. T. Waugh Collection 28, 80, 100
R. L. Wilson 70-74

Front endpapers: Two 1930s adverts depicting vehicles that ran on SMT's Edinburgh-London service. The 1932 AEC advert shows two of a batch of 11 1931 AEC Regals with 28-seat Cowieson bodies. The Burlingham advert dates from 1933, and shows one of six 28-seat AEC Regal coaches delivered that year.

Previous pages: They're off — at Epsom on Derby Day the spectators use double-deckers from the Lancaster, Southend, Southdown and Eastern National fleets as temporary grandstands.

Right: Some of the body styles available in 1963 on Ford Trader chassis, from a contemporary trade advert.

First published 1979

ISBN 0 7110 0934 1

Published by Ian Allan Ltd, Shepperton, Surrey; and printed in the United Kingdom by Ian Allan Printing Ltd

The Duple 'Trooper' 41 seater

The Duple 'Firefly' 41 seater

The Harrington 'Crusader' 41 seater

The Plaxton 'Embassy II' 41 seater

The Yeates 'Fiesta' 41 seater

The Martin Walter 25/29 seater

The Thurgood 'Forerunner' 28 seater

Contents

Introduction

At the close of another decade, *Buses Annual 1980* looks at the transport scene yesterday and today in a selection of articles and photo-features by some of the best-known writers and photographers around.

We go back to the 1920s for the birth of long-distance coaching, described by Charles F. Klapper, and also take a particular look at coach services between Scotland and London. Still on coaching, Ray Stenning looks at the fine bodies produced latterly by Harrington, and a photo-feature portrays some of the less familiar coach bodies of recent years.

The vehicles of Yorkshire Traction are illustrated in a G. H. F Atkins photo-feature, and the buses used by the municipal fleets that made up Selnec PTE are shown in R. L. Wilson photographs.

Electric traction is not forgotten. Michael Dryhurst looks back at London Transport's trolleybus conversion programme, and Robert E. Jowitt waxes lyrical about the tramcars — and other delights — of Portugal.

Looking at the motor bus itself, David Kaye pays tribute to the Bedford VAL chassis, and Martin J. Perry photographs recall the unfortunate Daimler Roadliner. D. Fereday Glenn turns his camera on bus interiors, rarely illustrated in books like this, and we look at non-standard examples of that highly-standardised species, the Leyland National.

Around Britain we have a feature on the services in and around the new town of Telford, by A. Moyes, on the buses which use Heathrow Airport, pictured by Stewart MacDonald, and on Tyne & Wear PTE, by G. Coxon.

The determination of Ulsterbus, against difficult odds, is described by R. C. Ludgate, and we travel around the world for Robert Grieves's recollections of bus driving in Australia.

The expert camera of T. W. Moore focuses on the buses which annually bring spectators to the Derby at Epsom, and several photographers have contributed to a photo-feature showing buses coping with adverse weather conditions.

To complete the *Annual* selection, Stewart J. Brown surveys the 49 local authority bus fleets remaining in Britain today, John Aldridge remembers some of the transport events he attended as a journalist, and Alan Millar appropriately looks back at Britain's buses in the 1970s.

Gavin Booth
Edinburgh

Adventurers on the Great North Road

GAVIN BOOTH looks back over 50 years of coach services between Scotland and London, at the many operators and their varied vehicles.

One of SBG's Supercoaches for the Scotland-London services, a Western SMT Volvo B58 with Alexander M type 42-seat body.

'Sir,' wrote Dr Johnson, 'the noblest prospect that a Scotchman ever sees, is the high road that leads him to London.' Mind you, he was prejudiced. And English, For years now, though, transport operators have been keen to encourage Scots to enjoy that prospect — and to show Englishmen the even nobler prospects awaiting them in Scotland. The fight for this traffic continues to this day, with road, rail and air services vying for the custom between London and Central Scotland, a journey of roughly 400 miles where prestige is almost as important as profit.

Today the fastest journey between Edinburgh or Glasgow and London is the 70min of the British Airways Shuttle or British Caledonian services, although British Rail has concentrated a great deal of investment on its east and west coast lines, with Inter-City 125s from Edinburgh since 1978, and first Electric Scots, and, more recently, the prototype Advanced Passenger Train sets from Glasgow. The complex air and rail cut-price fare scales now mean that at certain times the journeys can be cheap as well as fast, but consistently the cheapest means of public transport from Scotland to London have been the coaches of Scottish Bus Group, and speed hasn't been ignored with the growth of the country's motorway system.

Through coach services have operated between Scotland and London for 50 years, and it is necessary to go back to the Scottish Bus Group's predecessor, the SMT group, to discover the origins. London was an obvious goal for the fast-growing SMT company. From its first unsteady steps in 1906, William Thomson's brainchild had emerged as a healthy youngster, and the SMT network was spreading slowly but surely, from Edinburgh. Glasgow was reached in 1926, Newcastle in 1928, Carlisle in 1929 and Lancashire in 1930.

The main line railway companies had eventually been permitted to obtain interests in bus companies in 1928, and the availability of extra capital combined with the growing comfort and reliability of motor coaches helped to bring about a spectacular advance in long-distance coaching.

It was an English operator which offered the first through connection by coach to Scotland from London, when in 1928 Orange Bros of Bedlington advertised a link from its London-Newcastle services via the SMT/United route to Edinburgh. Other operators in the north-east of England were equally active. Majestic Saloon Coaches and National Coachways extended their London-Newcastle services to Edinburgh and Glasgow for a while, and Orange Bros eventually extended one day and one night coach right through via Edinburgh to Glasgow. County Motor Services of Stakeford also held a Glasgow-London licence for a time until taken over by United and SMT in 1932.

The looseness of some of the pre-Road Traffic Act licensing has clouded exact details of Scotland-London services around 1930. Many of the services did not involve through facilities, and it is suspected that many ceased to operate after the new Traffic Commissioners took over in 1931.

We do know that Amos Proud, Choppington, advertised an Edinburgh-London service, stopping overnight in Newcastle, from August 1927, and that following take-over by SMT the facility continued to be advertised. We also know that SMT sought to extend its Edinburgh-Berwick service to London via Doncaster in summer, and this was granted in 1929 — although it is doubtful if this was operated as a through service.

From the Scottish end, it was one of SMT's rivals which got to London first. Thomson's Tours started a daytime service between Edinburgh and London in 1929, using some impressive-looking normal control Daimler CF6s. The fare was 30s (£1.50). Thomson's had plans to introduce 40-seat Daimler double-deck sleeper coaches on the route in 1930, but the whole venture was to prove short-lived, and SMT took the service over on 11 April 1930. Although Thomson's had proposed a £1 single fare, the SMT fare was set at 30s and remained at this level for many years.

An SMT publication of 1931, *From London Town to Bonnie Scotland* points a romantic picture of early long-distance coach travel. It suggested that the motor coach was 'the luxurious modern equivalent of the old four-in-hand' and continued in the same vein: 'We board the motor-coach at Lupus Street Coastal Coaches Station, and after settling down in the comfortable and well-sprung seats, we are off! Not mere "passengers for Edinburgh", but adventurers on the Great North Road!'

With an accompanying map it traces the route to the north, past the site of the Battle of Barnet ('where steel clashed on steel and the fortunes of dynasties were swayed!'), through the rural Home Counties, now somewhat changed by more than 40 years of ribbon development, passing Baldock ('this quiet English hamlet') and an 'aeroplane ground' near Wansford, before stopping at Stoke Rochford Road House ('a delightful establishment under the able management of Captain Elms, where a halt for lunch is made'). The coach forges north, through Civil War country, past Doncaster and through 'a smiling countryside dotted at intervals with villages' to Darlington, where 'a refreshing interval occurs for tea'.

After Newcastle's industrial shapes ('which combine to make a not inharmonious whole') the coach heads across to Wooler and the unhappy memories of Flodden. 'Flodden Field!' exclaims the writer, 'The name still falls upon the ear like the note of a passing bell borne down the corridor of the centuries!'

Across the border at Coldstream, the coach heads to Greenlaw, a town 'awakened to new life with the revival of coach-travel'. Through 'the quiet streets of Dalkeith', the coach reaches the end of its 15-hour journey in Edinburgh, with the castle 'a cluster of lights high in the darkness, seeming like some fairy citadel suspended in air'.

Romantic stuff — but this was 1931, when the prospect of that 386-mile journey was more daunting than it is today.

The first Glasgow-London connection was made via Edinburgh and Newcastle, by extending existing services. The first through service from Glasgow was operated by Midland Bus Services of Airdrie. SMT had acquired Midland in 1929, and soon afterwards a direct service started via Carlisle and Scotch Corner. On 10 March 1932, the day that Victoria Coach Station opened in London, Midland attracted a great deal of publicity by running a new oil-engined AEC Regal to Glasgow in 16hr 32min, at an average speed of 26.5mph. The oil engine was then very new in buses, and the SMT group's initiative helped its widespread acceptance. Midland disappeared into the newly-formed Western SMT later in 1932, and the red Midland coaches gave way to the blue and then black and white of Western. This helped to avoid confusion at Victoria Coach Station, where the existence of Midland *red* coaches and Midland *Red* coaches caused at least one old lady to ask the way to Smethwick — on arrival in Glasgow.

Back on the east coast, a two-day sightseeing Edinburgh-London service was introduced by SMT in 1930. Thomson's had pioneered a three-day tour in 1925 and a two-day run was advertised in 1928. Scott's 'Azure Blue' coaches followed with a two-day service in 1930, and this continued until taken over by SMT in 1932. Eventually SMT and its post-

On the Orange Bros London-Glasgow service at Grantham in 1933, a 1932 Maudslay Meteor with Strachan 26-seat body which in 1934 passed to SMT with a share of the Orange business.

Grantham again, but in 1935 with a Western SMT all-Leyland Tiger TS7 32-seater leaving for Glasgow.

nationalisation successor Scottish Omnibuses, operated two, three and four-day sightseeing services between Scotland and London by various routes, and the two- and three-day survive today as a convenient way for overseas tourists to 'do' Oxford, Stratford, Chester and the Lake District while travelling to Scotland.

In 1934 Orange Bros was taken over by United, and the services north of Newcastle were withdrawn to leave the road clear for SMT.

By 1937, with the fare still at 30s, the London services from Edinburgh and Glasgow were continuing their successful expansion. A bus timetable of that year describes the Edinburgh-London service as 'the only non-stop express service between Scotland and London' — in spite of meal stops totalling 40min. Coaches left Edinburgh at 07.30 and 17.30, reaching Victoria 15hr 19min later.

At first the vehicles used by SMT and Midland on London services were selected from the best of their own and acquired fleets. Then the first of many batches of special London coaches were bought. Late in the summer of 1930, SMT placed in service six Leyland Tiger TS2s with luxurious 27-seat

Burlingham bodies, and four similar coaches went to Midland. The next year the SMT fleet was augmented by 12 28-seat Cowieson-bodied AEC Regal coaches, all but one bought new; the twelfth coach was a 1930 AEC demonstrator which lost its original Strachan bus body.

Then there were Midland's three 1932 AEC Regal oilers with Wycombe bodies, and from 1933 several of the Leyland Tiger TS3s formerly with Premier Line, were used. Western bought 20 Wycombe-bodied Gilford Hera coaches in 1934, and some of these were used for a time on Glasgow-London, although, like the Premier Line Tigers and the AEC Regals, they were relatively short-lived in the fleet and were withdrawn after as little as three years' service.

SMT stuck to AECs for its next London batch, six Burlingham-bodied oil-engined Regals delivered for the 1933 summer season; they introduced what was to become a standard feature on Scotland-London coaches, a rear toilet compartment. Following the takeover of Orange Bros, several coaches passed to the SMT fleet, and one, a Weymann-bodied 1933 AEC Regal, was used on the London service by SMT.

After its flirtation with Gilfords, Western stuck

firmly with Leylands for all of its new full-size vehicles from 1935-40. Among these were 29 Tiger TS7s with 32-seat Leyland coach bodies, new in 1935 and used on Glasgow-London, and a batch of 15 Burlingham-bodied full-fronted TS7s licensed, for some reason, over three seasons from 1937-39.

In 1936 SMT also took Burlingham-bodied Tiger TS7s, ornate dark blue coaches with full-fronts, 22 well-spaced seats, and toilet accommodation. These were granted the extra distinction of names from the novels of Sir Walter Scott, and were the mainstay of the SMT London route until the outbreak of war, but some of the 1937 batch of Duple-bodied Tiger TS7s also performed on the service.

After war broke out in 1939, the London services continued to operate for a few months, but were soon withdrawn as 'non-essential'. Many of the special London coaches were withdrawn and rebodied as double-deckers during the war years, so the SMT 1933 Regals and 1936 Tigers, and most of the Western Tiger TS7s all re-emerged with lowbridge Alexander bodies between 1942 and 1945.

Special coaches were difficult to obtain when the services were reinstated after the war, so early postwar standard coaches were used until essential vehicle replacement and rebuilding could be completed, and thoughts could turn to special vehicles.

SMT's London services restarted in 1946 with new Duple-bodied AEC Regals from a batch of 50 coaches, and continued with Alexander-bodied Regals from 1947/48 batches. Western tackled the situation differently, and collected 30 Leyland Lion LT5As from various sources which in 1946 received new Brush 30-seat coach bodies. These were joined in 1948/49 by new Burlingham-bodied coaches, a handful of short-lived Daimler CVD6s, and a number of Leyland Tiger PS1s. None of these coaches was fitted out as luxuriously as their prewar brothers, nor did the SMT coaches have toilets, but they helped re-establish the services.

The arrival of a competitor on the Scotland-London services prompted SMT, now re-titled Scottish Omnibuses Ltd, and Western SMT to re-equip their fleets. The competition came from the Glasgow-based independent firm of Northern Roadways, with a fleet of Burlingham-bodied AEC Regal IVs and Leyland Royal Tigers. The overnight Northern Roadways services from Glasgow and Edinburgh to London by 'Pullman de-luxe sleeper night coaches' cost £2 single (the SOL/Western fare was still 30s) — but this included 'hostess snacks'.

To combat this competiton, in 1951 SMT ordered 40 AEC Regal IVs with special Alexander 30-seat bodies, but new stock was also urgently required by Western, and 14, with Edinburgh registration

numbers, were diverted for use on the Glasgow-London service. The Regal IVs featured reclining seats, individual reading lights and toilet accommodation, and these quiet, smooth-running coaches were popular performers on the services from Scotland to London. SOL bought more Regal IVs in 1953, but Western turned to Guy Arab UF and LUF models. The Western London fleet tended to be replaced more regularly, but the SOL Regal IVs lasted on the London run until 1966, by which time several had completed over one million miles in service.

The Western Regal IVs were re-seated as buses in 1955, by which time several batches of Guy Arab UFs had been placed in service on the London run. The first 11, delivered in 1953 as 36-seaters, were soon converted to 30-seat toilet coaches, and these were followed by another five later the same year. These had Alexander centre-entrance Coronation-style bodies. In 1954/55 the lighter-weight Guy Arab LUF was specified, with front entrance 30-seat bodies; the 20 coaches involved were reseated to 41, without toilets, in 1960 on the arrival of 20 Leyland Leopard L1s with 30-seat Alexander bodies. The Leopards — the Scottish Bus Group's first — were 30ft models, the current legal maximum length, but when 36ft single-deckers were permitted from 1961, one of the first was a long AEC Reliance coach with the prototype of what was to become the Alexander Y type body. This 38-seat coach eventually joined the SOL fleet, and was followed by six similar Reliances in 1963. At the same time, Western chose 16 similarly-bodied Leyland Leopards.

The 36ft SOL Reliances replaced some of the Regal IVs, and were in fact the company's first new London coaches for 10 years, apart from one 30-seat AEC Reliance built in 1955.

The 36ft Alexander Y type body, with seats for 38 and toilet accommodation, was specified for the next London coaches, the first on rear-engined chassis. These were Bristol RELH6Gs in 1966, 33 for SOL, now carrying the Eastern Scottish fleetname, and 21 for Western.

Meantime, there had been advances in the services themselves. Although the fares had slowly but inevitably crept up, the timings had been improved. The M6 and M1 motorways enabled Eastern Scottish and Western to slash their timings quite dramatically. The fastest Eastern Scottish time, using the motorway network, came down to $9\frac{1}{2}$ hours, while Western, with the added benefit of faster roads within Scotland, has reduced its fastest time to $8\frac{1}{2}$ hours.

These faster limits have brought the rest of Scotland into closer contact with London. First in 1973 existing services were linked to provide through facilities; the Eastern Scottish Edinburgh-London service was

Two Northern Roadways AEC Regal IVs with centre entrance Burlingham Seagull bodywork prepare to leave Kings Cross coach station for Glasgow.

SMT answered the Northern Roadways challenge with a fleet of Alexander-bodied AEC Regal IVs in 1951. Part of a convoy is seen en route to Edinburgh.

The first 12metre Bristol REMH/Alexander coach for SBG loads at Edinburgh on its first trip to London. It was then painted in an unusual black and yellow livery.

linked across the Forth with Glenrothes, Kirkcaldy and Dunfermline; the Glasgow-London was linked with the existing Glasgow-Aberdeen licence to provide a through Aberdeen-London facility. Eastern and Western coaches worked right through on both services in 1973, but in 1974, when direct services were granted from Fife and Aberdeen, Eastern and Western London coaches were operated on hire by Alexanders (Fife) and Alexanders (Northern).

The Fife and Northern companies received their own coaches early in 1975, in time for the new season. The coaches were Leyland Leopards, but with the unusual Alexander M type body, first introduced in 1968. After several years of adapting existing Alexander designs for its London fleet, the bus group decided that its 1968-70 intake of London coaches should be purpose-built, and should be to the newly-legalised length of 39ft 4in (12m). The impressive M type body with its small high-set double-glazed windows was the result, and was first built on Bristol REMH6G for Eastern (8) and Western (16) in 1968/69. The reclining seats were well-spaced, with two pairs of seats to each window bay, and the standard of interior fitment was high, with individual reading lights and forced-air ventilation, and the normal toilet accommodation.

The Eastern coaches were painted in an unusual yellow and black livery, while Western stuck to its traditional black and white colours. Eastern added

another 25 REMH6G/M types in 1970, and Western received a further 21 in 1971. The next M types for SBG were 1975 deliveries, the Leopards already mentioned for Fife (3) and Northern (6), and three for Eastern — although they worked from Edinburgh for only a matter of months before being diverted, one to Fife and two to Northern. Western also received new M types in 1975, and these were unique in the Bus Group as they were on Volvo B58 chassis.

The only other London coaches to be built were six M types for Eastern Scottish on Seddon Pennine 7 chassis in 1976, and these were delivered in the group's corporate blue and white SCOTTISH livery, adopted earlier that year to replace the four different liveries now in evidence on SBG coaches, and to reinforce the group's identity, particularly in the south in a sea of all-white National coaches.

Since then extra pick-up points have been added, and Western has extended some of its Glasgow timings to start from the Clyde resorts of Dunoon and Rothesay. Other important Scottish towns which have recently received direct connections with Scotland include Greenock, Paisley, East Kilbride, Hamilton, Livingston, Cumbernauld and Falkirk.

The group's fleet of blue and white M type coaches on the main roads and motorways of Britain are an impressive sight, and a far cry from the 16-hour journeys of the 1930s.

10

Epsom Assaults

Derby Day at Epsom Racecourse is an important day for racing enthusiasts — and for bus enthusiasts too, for a fascinating selection of buses and coaches brings the spectators. Photographs by T. W. MOORE.

Above: Watching the 1978 Derby from the top decks of buses at Epsom, in this case an East Kent AEC Regent V/Park Royal, a Southdown Leyland Titan PD3/Northern Counties and an Eastern National Bristol K/ECW.

Left: What's up, Doc? Lunch on the front nearside wing of 'Doc', one of Lancaster City's open-top Leyland Titan PD2/37s.

11

The Punters are happy after lunch, and the bookies are happy, at least until after the race. The bus is an ex-Southampton Guy Arab, resting after its long drive to Epsom.

A more modern open-topper arrives at Epsom, a smartly-painted Devon General Bristol VRT3 with ECW body.

Arrival at Epsom after enduring the inevitable traffic jams, a Southdown Bristol FS6B with ECW body, new in 1960 to Brighton, Hove & District.

'Western Conqueror' reaches the racecourse. It is one of the 1961 Bristol/ECW FS6Gs from the Bristol Omnibus fleet.

13

Above: Not quite 'Open-Top to the Zoo', but an animal spectacle of a different kind. One of the ex-Midland Red D9s from Prince Marshall's Obsolete Fleet reaches Epsom.

Left: Open rear staircases are unusual on buses at Derby Day — but then they're not exactly commonplace on former London Transport RTs either. This amusing conversion was carried out on RT2461 to widen its appeal for overseas tourists.

Right: A sit-down strike by spectators, refusing to budge even for this Hants & Dorset Bristol VRT — one of the problems created by the late arrival of some of the buses.

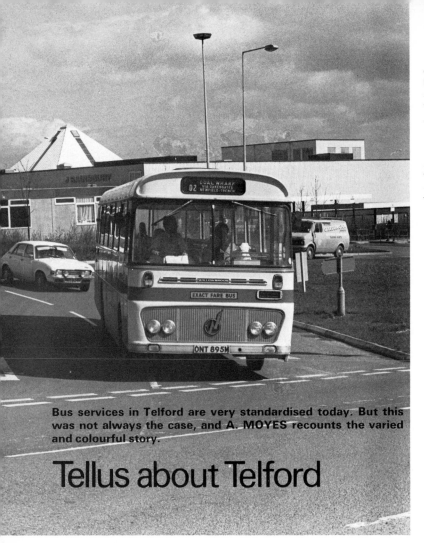

Bus services in Telford are very standardised today. But this was not always the case, and A. MOYES recounts the varied and colourful story.

Tellus about Telford

Some things, they say, are too good to last. Bus operation in east Shropshire presumably fell into this situation until recently, as far as most students of transport are concerned. As is well known, on 1 April 1978 the National Bus Company at last obtained an almost complete hold on local stage carriage bus operation by taking over all but one of the surviving locally-based urban bus operators, members of the Shropshire Omnibus Association. At a stroke, variety was replaced by conformity. Although the NBC's local representative Midland Red boldly applied the local 'brand name' of 'Tellus' (presumably a more catchy term than 'Telbus') to its allocation at Wellington depot, this

is poor consolation for the vernacular interest and identity of what preceded it. Here it is hoped to convey something of the distinctive flavour of the independents' hold on short-distance urban operation in the east Shropshire conurbation of Telford not so long ago, and of the sadly blander dish which is now on offer.

The new town of Telford derives its name from Thomas Telford, the famous engineer who in the early 19th century was the Shropshire county surveyor, and who was responsible for many improvements in roads and bridges both locally and internationally. The East Shropshire coalfield was one of the cradles of the Industrial Revolution, at an early

date accumulating a heavy industrial base and a string of loosely-knit settlements, which were to form three parallel, broadly west-to-east zones. The northernmost developed into a lowland sliver of industry and urbanisation abutting on to the flat north Shropshire plain, and contained the old market town of Wellington and the newer, duller town of Oakengates. Next, south of Thomas Telford's reconstructed London-Holyhead road, lay an undulating, upraised plateau, shallowly underlain with coal, pockmarked with derelict land and housing clusters. Some of these were small towns, like Dawley, others a few terraced rows, like Old Park or Mannerley Lane. Between them would be occasional opencast clay pits or ironworks. On this zone's southern edge, it was sharply bounded by the early-industrialised but beautiful, wooded Severn gorge, containing such settlements as Coalbrookdale (where iron was first smelted using coke, by Abraham Darby), and the appropriately-named Ironbridge — settlements sufficiently matured to have dignity. The industrial momentum of the area lagged; by the 1930s, the coal, iron and to a lesser extent clay industries were decaying and depressed. The economy was stablised just before World War II by the establishment of a huge military storage depot in the north-east of the incipient conurbation at Donnington. But major growth did not begin until some 30 years later. Stemming from a small-scale overspill agreement between Birmingham and the then Dawley Urban District, the whole conurbation was designated a new town, and steps taken to cohere the whole area into a home for 250,000 people. By 1978, partly by overspill of people and jobs from the West Midlands conurbation some 20 miles away, Telford had almost 100,000 residents, and the landscape, particularly of the central zone of the town, had been metaphorically and literally reshaped, by land clearance, new neighbourhood units, writhing urban motorways whose logic is as yet not always clear, and a new town centre which bids fair to become of regional

Left: H. Brown's 60-seat Bedford YRT/Willowbrook pulls away from the Telford bus station in March 1978, bound for the Coal Wharf at Donnington.

Below: Midland Red's Wellington allocation includes a number of the Ford/Plaxton buses. Here one approaches Oakengates past Maddock's foundry, on the Little Dawley route.

importance.

In the 1920s, most of the numerous small bus operators who germinated in the area's promising soil tried their luck on one or other of the then two main traffic axes — from Wellington to Donnington, or to Oakengates and beyond it to Wrockwardine Wood. Not unusually, when the Road Traffic Bill of 1929 threatened the future of the smaller operators vis-a-vis the expansive Midland Red, a local small-men's association was formed, the Mid-Shropshire Omnibus Association. In 1931 this association was absorbed by a newly-formed Shropshire Omnibus Association Limited, with a capital of £1,000. Among its first directors were names like Williams,

Price, Hoggins, Brown, Smith and Jones, which were long to grace the local bus scene.

The association's main work was to devise and manage two rotas, one for each of the trunk routes. By means of these, vehicles of participating members would perform similar running schedules during — initially — one-month (but in later years three-month) periods. In effect, vehicle and associated crew duties were allocated to, and circulated among operators. Because participants could expect to obtain a fair share of the revenue on their route in the long term, fares were kept by operators, rather than pooled as in most other co-operative schemes. Full members paid a

subscription based on their share in the rota; these were used to pay for tickets and punches, the production and publishing of an association timetable, and for administrative expenses such as the burdensome clerical task of relicensing each rota when it changed hands monthly (later quarterly). At first, there were 16 operators on the Oakengates-Wrockwardine Wood rota, and 14 on the Wellington-Donnington one. As each required a basic six or so vehicles, clearly there were long idle periods for some participants. Midland Red ran on both routes too, in a co-ordinated but administratively separate fashion, at a rate of some two BMMO vehicles to every five Shropshire Omnibus

An ageing Bedford SB/Duple Bella Vega of Elcock, Ironbridge carries the morning shift from Granville colliery, on Telford's eastern edge, back home to Broseley in June 1978.

membership to local small operators of stage services on other, non-rota routes, and of contracts, excursions and tours; for them, a reduced subscription applied. By 1950 there were 19 such non-rota members. The most notable departure from their ranks was perhaps Hoggins in January 1974, passing his Oakengates-Dawley route to Midland Red. But by 1978 there were ony two operators of non-rota stage services surviving in the conurbation. The larger, with seven vehicles, was J. Ashley of Dawley, running circuitously thence to Wellington approximately hourly via the New Town Centre and Mannerley Lane. He also had a Thursday-only variant via Lawley Bank, some works and school contracts and, amongst other activities, a regular shoppers' excursion to Wolverhampton. The other was G. E. Smith (Britannia) of Wrockwardine Wood, running an hourly Oakengates-Lawley Bank-New Town Centre-Dawley route. However, three rota operators had other routes exclusively to themselves. The thrice hourly Donnington-Oakengates-Town Centre service of H. Brown was much more important in vehicular equipments than his share in the Wellington-Donnington rota, and he also had a skein of market-day services taking his cream and green vehicles as far as Newport and Market Drayton. Secondly, Martlew ran a series of Donnington-Town Centre-Shifnal services which were in effect long-standing publicly-timed works services, in part serving the new Stafford Park industrial estate. Finally, Smith's Eagle provided a Thursdays-only circular south-west from Wellington into delightful rural countryside, to Cressage. This was a relatively recent extension of an existing market-day license from Wellington to a spot on the flanks of the Wrekin, the massive abrupt hill which dominates Telford's western edge. Before car-borne leisure motoring robbed them of patrons, three SOA members used to run 'on demand' services on weekends and Bank Holidays, to a cafe on the hillside.

As regards route abandonments,

Association (SOA).

Initially, few SOA rota members had more than one vehicle. Any member wishing to sell out could do so only to another member of the same rota, though a few transgressions were later to occur. By 1966 there were only four members of the Donnington rota, and five on the Wrockwardine Wood rota, on each of which, however, one member dominated. In October 1973 the first major incursion into the system occurred with the sale of the quite large business of Cooper, Oakengates, to Midland Red. At the end of SOA in early 1978, the Donnington quartet remained as Martlew and A.T. Brown each with two shares, H. Brown with one, and

Smith's Eagle with six (from two sources other than its own original share). The dominant operator covering the Wrockwardine Wood rota routes was, paradoxically, Midland Red with the equivalent of four shares, all of them ex-Cooper but of which one had originated with Hoggins and the other with E. D. Smith; these, of course, excluded the long-standing aloof pair of Midland Red vehicles on this service. The Wrockwardine Wood rota members proper were Price's Excelsior with two shares and C. E. Williams with one; the latter's vehicle was actually operated for it by Martlew, from the Donnington rota.

From its beginning, SOA offered

A Leyland National on Midland Red's only involvement in colliery specials in Telford, bouncing over the potholed lane past Granville Colliery's upcast shaft in June 1978.

there were only two major retractions by members. In 1971 C. E. Williams' market day route from Wrockwardine Wood to Newport lapsed, and in the mid-1970s the thin weekday service along the Severn gorge from the dying village at Coalport through Ironbridge to its local authority estate perched above the gorge at Hodge Bower also ceased. A. L. Jones of Madeley had run this under the title of Victoria Coaches, but after six years' control by Smith's Eagle, the title of Telford Coaches was adopted in 1970, and kept by Elcock of Ironbridge when he took over in late 1973. This operator still runs some workmen's services to the area's last surviving colliery, a

somewhat discreetly located affair east of the conurbation at St Georges, and he also runs a shuttle service between various industrial museum sites along the Severn gorge on behalf of the Ironbridge Museum Trust. To summarise, then, by early 1978 there were still eight SOA members running bus services wholly within the urban area.

Arising from the association's success in the stage carriage field, it hived off a Contract Services Association in 1950, to co-ordinate rates for private hires. A similar organisation arose in the late 1960s under the title of Wrekin Coach Services Ltd to co-ordinate the growing amount of coaching and

extended tour business which the new town was generating. These associations were able to negotiate large-scale arrangements when demand arose, and call on some 25 to 30 vehicles, as readily as an area-agreement operator.

For the average passenger, SOA meant relatively little directly. It made no attempt to influence members' choice of vehicles, liveries or ticket systems, unlike some Associations elsewhere. The most casual glance through the PSV Circle — Omnibus Society's fleet history of the Shropshire independents confirms that SOA members were truly independent as far as vehicle policy was concerned. Many purchased new coaches, some

19

turning them over frequently, others (though less so in recent years) frugally. Of late, this led to some rota passengers enjoying the latest coachwork by Caetano, Duple or Plaxton. These could be regarded as heirs to the large ageing batches of Metalcraft-bodied Crossleys running for many years with Cooper, or H. Brown's rare all-Sentinel coaches. Rather fewer kept studs of buses, some favouring new, others second-hand, some short-lived, others long-serving. One could contrast H. Brown's trio of Dutfield-bodied Vulcans which faithfully plodded to such distinctive destinations as Trench, Humbers, Bell Gate and Coal Wharf for the 1950 decade, with the 'one of everything second hand' fleet of Ashley, or with the Bedford OWBs of Smith's Eagle which were still running in utilitarian splendour till 1967. The SOA's secretary, Mr Tranter, confessed to a correspondent from *Commercial Motor* in 1953 that he felt there might be advantages for the association in standardising on 40-seat buses and a common livery — possibly of blue and black, to match the SOA letter-headings! He may have had in mind as a standard the Sentinel STC4/40, produced just down the road in Shrewsbury. Alone of the locals, H. Brown was an enthusiastic Sentinel user, proving their potential by hanging on to a pair of the rare coach versions until 1974. Wonderful, chortling machines, they were. Whatever standardisation arose latterly was enforced, by the narrowing choice of models available. The Bedford VAM and YRQ, almost invariably Willowbrook-bodied, was a general choice for the relatively few service buses which members bought new in the 1970s, though H. Brown had two mighty 60-seat YRTs; Price and Hoggins each indulged in a Ford/Plaxton bus, mimicking Midland Red's flurry of interest in lightweights. In vehicular terms, the most interesting SOA fleet at the end was Smith's Eagle's; a Bedford SB/Duple Midland bus VTG 739 which had begun life with Thomas, Barry and which was eagerly snapped up by Warstone, Great

Wyrley for stage use; an intact 1949 Commer Commando/Harrington coach, and elderly Duple Britannia-bodied AEC Reliance coaches. Ashley had two interesting specimens: a battered Bedford SB/Strachan bus previously with Bebb, Llantwit Fadre, and possibly the first (and not far from the last) Ford with Marshall bus bodywork, new to York Bros of Northampton. But the variety of liveries ensured that even the more mundane modern coaches of SOA were distinctive.

As mentioned, the purchase of Cooper by Midland Red in October 1973 was the first serious incursion into SOA integrity. At the time it was hinted that negotiations for sale were afoot with other SOA members, several of whom were approaching retirement age. Midland Red was about to lose its large and worthwhile Black Country operations to the West Midlands PTE. It considered that county councils were increasingly likely to subsidise bus operations and was therefore more willing than previously to take over companies (like Green Bus not far away) which were not necessarily highly profitable. It was keen to consolidate its hold on its existing operating area, thus sustaining its traditional scale of operation despite losing 400-odd vehicles elsewhere. There is little doubt that both the county council and the New Town Development Corporation favoured a tidier pattern of bus ownership in Telford, feeling that a more sensible pattern of operation linking old and new areas of the town could thereby be achieved. At first the corporation merely allocated route numbers to the independents, which were not often displayed. As the new town developed, particularly on the opening of the first shops in the town centre, friction arose as to how new services were to be pooled. Midland Red had traditionally covered the southern part of Telford and those new neighbourhood units built by then; the SOA members mainly covered the northern area and had access to the town centre only by almost two miles of urban motorway with no intervening traffic potential. Though some

Wrockwardine Wood rota services and some H. Brown trips were extended to the centre, the outcome was not satisfactory and much duplicate running ensued. Nevertheless, news of Midland Red's completion of negotiations and of a new pattern of services and routes was sudden. In early 1978 it was announced that all SOA's stage activities (except for those of Price) would cease with effect from 1 April 1978, Midland Red reportedly paying £$\frac{1}{2}$m for them. At the same time, non-stage work in the area would fall almost exclusively to the independents. The rapidity of the change was such that the Traffic Commissioners had little time to ratify Midland Red's proposed schedules and fares before the take-over. Ironically, objections by old SOA members were to delay the advent of Travelcard and other promotional fares on the new network, until some weeks after it began to operate. On 1 April, the era of the urban independent bus in East Shropshire came virtually to an end; only a solitary Price vehicle, shuttling each hour on the Wellington-Donnington section, remained thereafter. And, unlike the earlier Midland Red acquisitions, not a single SOA vehicle was involved in the deal.

It is indicative of the previously rather low level of vehicle utilisation that, despite the takeover of SOA's bus commitments, Midland Red's Wellington depot should have an unchanged allocation of 51, for the new schedules. Though 20 brand-new Leyland Nationals arrived, they replaced an equivalent number of own-make S17 saloons, The whole bus allocation — also including S23s, various Leyland Leopard/Willowbrook machines, and Fords — received the now-familiar white cantrail band in Fablon, bearing the local brand-name, in this case, 'Tellus'. The new route network incorporating the independents' work needed a basic 18 vehicles off-peak compared with almost 35 laid aside by both parties for the equivalent work previously. The main features of the new route pattern was the linking of acquired and existing routes to give longer,

A Shropshire Education Department Bedford VAS passes the iron bridge at Ironbridge in March 1978 — apparently giving the local war memorial a lift to the Abraham Darby school.

sometimes circular routes with reduced layover and turnround time. Hence, most of the Donnington rota trips were linked with the former H. Brown's Donnington-Oakengates-Town Centre facilities, as routes 914 and 915. About half of the former Wrockwardine Wood rota trips were diverted from their long-standing terminus at St Georges New Yard, to the New Town Centre, and thence prolonged into hitherto pure Midland Red country to Madeley and one of the new residental areas at Woodside (route 921). Other bits were re-shaped to cover further ex-H. Brown variants in Wrockwardine Wood. Two existing Oakengates-Dawley routes were ingeniously matched with other Midland Red services to Madeley and the same Woodside neighbourhood unit, and extended at their northern ends to Wellington. These were respectively

a part-replacement for the ex-Smith's Britannia Oakengates-Dawley route via an even more contorted sequence of roads than previously (as route 901), and the ex-Hoggins route between these points via Mannerley Lane (route 920). The final major innovation was that Ashley's two routes from Wellington to Dawley were neatly used to channel most of Midland Red's existing frequent trips from Wellington to Dawley, Madeley and the first of the Development Corporation's estates at Sutton Hill, away from the thinly-populated Wellington-Dawley main road used hitherto; these took route numbers 907 and 908.

On the debit side, the older parts of the designated area, such as Horsehay, Coalbrookdale and Ironbridge, suffered reduced frequencies, almost symbolically reflecting the movement of the town's centre of gravity northwards and eastwards. However, longer-distance routes in the area were now more closely dovetailed with the in-town services, giving more even headways. Links between Wellington and Much Wenlock,

Bridgnorth and Newport were particularly affected. The latter involved Shrewsbury depot also, as did Shrewsbury-Wolverhampton stage and express services.

What then remains for the enthusiast visiting Telford? Midland Red's Wellington allocation is not particularly distinguished, other than by the waning numbers of own-make saloons. The old Donnington rota route is still served by one Price vehicle shuttling along the A518 every hour and obediently carrying route number 916. This is by no means a scenic route, but it does pass two old SOA members' depots at Trench, namely of A. T. Brown and Smith's Eagle. At Donnington at rush hours may be glimpsed specimens of the Price, Martlew and Smith's Britannia fleets emerging from the Central Ordnance Depot on contract work. And here, at the dismal bus station, one meets end-on the quite important route from Stafford run by G. H. Austin's 'Happy Days' business; he also runs right into Wellington on a main road, twice daily rail replacement service from Stafford, and an indirect affair from Newport via Cherrington on Thursdays into Wellington's Haygate Road. That day also sees C. H. Butter coming in from Childs Ercall to the more convenient Charlton Street, right by the Midland Red depot, but with unremarkable Bedford coaches. In the central zone of Telford, the interests are more scenic than vehicular, though for the more wayward tastes. On routes 901 and 920, for instance, the sinuous routing is enlivened by the 'level crossings' where massive dump trucks working on land reclamation and clay extraction move from site to site, flagged through by 'crossing keepers'. On the eastern edge of this zone, a panoply of Midland Red and other vehicles serves the Halesfield industrial estate at rush hours, though difficult to witness in their entirety because of the intricacies of the road network. The Severn gorge is almost monopolised by standard Midland Red types. What a pity that Midland Red could not have kept some ex-SOA vehicles and put them to work in this, the scenic high-spot of the new town! That would have been something worth telling.

Upstairs, Downstairs

D. FEREDAY GLENN

Left: Few double-deckers offered luggage-racks to their passengers, but Southern Vectis specified them for its final series of Bristol KSW5G lowbridge buses when it inherited certain former rail routes in the Isle of Wight in 1953. Eastern Coach Works 55-seat bodywork is fitted.

Below: The older and narrower ECW body on Hants & Dorset Bristol K6B 1230, again featuring the offside sunken gangway of the lowbridge layout that was a familiar feature on many of Britain's buses for many years.

SMOKING PROHIBITED

PLEASE LOWER YOUR HEAD

Upstairs on a lowbridge body, with the once-familiar four-abreast seating. The ECW body on Hants & Dorset 1265 dates from 1940, but the chassis is a decade younger. Note the ribbed roof and general utility finish, although the windows were rubber-mounted at a later stage.

Smokers and non-smokers were segregated even on the lower deck of Southdown's topless Leyland Titans. This is the downstairs view of the Brush body on 813, the preserved TD1.

A vintage look, but dating only from 1950. The one-off East Lancs rear-entrance body fitted to Eastbourne AEC Regal AHC 411. Ornate coach seats, Clayton heater and mirrors all suggest the 1930s, but the bus remained in service until 1976.

The standard ECW body on Bristol LS was a neat and effective design. This 1953 Hants & Dorset LS5G is seen after it had been attractively refurbished in the Wilts & Dorset bodyshop.

A backward look at the ECW body on Hants & Dorset Bristol L 680. The bus was new in 1950 with Portsmouth Aviation body, but received this body in 1962, and ended its days with Wilts & Dorset at Basingstoke.

Non-Standard Standards

That most standard of modern buses, the Leyland National, has also appeared in decidedly non-standard guises, and a few are shown on these pages. This is the prototype Super National Business Commuter, a luxuriously outfitted executive coach laden with electric and electronic gadgetry. It is seen here at Victoria coach station in London in 1974.

The National Bus mobile conference room National, at Kelvedon in 1975.

British Airways operates a fleet of these distinctly odd half-cab Nationals for airside transfers at Heathrow airport.

More normal — but with three doors — another British Airways National at Heathrow. With two nearside doors and an offside door they can be used as airside coaches or on normal highway duties.

At first glance a standard National, this was the prototype 10.9 metre bus, a mixture of 10.3 metre and 11.3 metre parts. It was eventually sold to the independent operator Rennies of Dunfermline, and fitted with coach seats.

FRM 499K, the tenth of Leyland's pre-production prototype Nationals, started life as a demonstrator, but in 1976 became a mobile service training school for the manufacturers.

Used as a mobile bank by the Midland Bank, JHV 611N is seen here in United's Whitby depot, where it is based and maintained, in 1978.

Old picture postcards have long been recognised as an important source of reference for transport enthusiasts. Railway trains, tramcars and buses frequently figure prominently in postcards, and this is the first of three selections from the collection of GEORGE F. T. WAUGH.

Top: The happy band of travellers in the Lancia charabanc may well have just arrived at Arrochar, but the doctoring of early postcards was such that the chara and the road only really met in the dark-room.

Right: A quiet day at Saltburn, with a 34-seat Highland Transport Albion SPW67 en route for Inverness.

The Square at Portknockie, Banffshire in the 1930s, with Alexanders N67, a 1931 Leyland Lion LT3 with 36-seat Alexander body.

Three Scottish Bus Group Leyland Leopards with Alexander
M type bodies outside the coachworks in 1975 wearing liveries
that were to prove short-lived with the introduction of the
corporate blue and white scheme. These vehicles belonged to
Alexanders (Fife), Alexanders (Northern) and Eastern Scottish.

Red Wine and Yellow Trams

Torn between these rival attractions ROBERT E. JOWITT describes the pleasures to be found in Portugal.

A Lisbon bogie car at Belem.

As soon as I emerge from the platform into the concourse of Santa Apolonia, the main station of Lisbon, I am approached by two men one after the other trying to sell me watches. As most of the way across Spain in the dark I was sitting on the floor of the vestibule I am now in no mood to buy a watch. Anyway I have a watch already. Moreover I have not come to Lisbon to buy a watch, I have come partly for reasons which, as Victorian novels say, need not concern my readers, and partly to read, mark, learn and inwardly digest, as the prayerbook or something says, the tramway system.

Most immediately, however, I find myself a room in the first *pensao* I encounter, several floors up in an ancient tenement building across the road from the station. This room has a basin with Portuguese plumbing peculiarities which flood my floor; also a population of ants who instal themselves eagerly in my loaf of bread. But it has a French window and a little balcony with a wonderful view of the shiping in the Tagus and the distant hills beyond the water, and it is the only room I have ever had in which I could lie in bed and look down upon the trams.

Delightful indolence though this is, I must not rest content but must explore Lisbon further . . .

The city was largely destroyed in 1755 by an earthquake, and rebuilt on, as far as was permitted by the nature of the terrain, a sensible plan by the Marquis of Pombal. (Pombal, incidentally, is translated 'Dovecot'.)

Lisbon is said, like Rome, to be set upon seven hills. Whether there are seven or more, their effect on the tramways is sensational: For example, take the top of the Alfama district, one of the few quarters of Lisbon undamaged by the earthquake and therefore retaining its medieval and Arabic nature. From the centre or lower part of the city the trams climb steeply, swinging wildly past the front of the Cathedral, to plunge into incredible alleys, so narrow in places that the canary cages hanging outside the windows of the houses seem at risk. One of the more fantastic torturings of tramline is the short route from São Tomé to Martim Moniz; this crosses a summit where the rails achieve no less than an inverted V, and then dives down almost vertically. On the route which continues up to Graça there are several blind or nearly blind corners, and as there is room only for single or at best interlaced track the blindest corners are controlled by signalmen. These signalmen are either fat old Portuguese or else young men of ferocious equatorial aspect, and they all sit on little stools outside taverns. One has an imposing interlaced rightangle all to himself; such an angle that if a descending tram derailed it would go straight into the tavern. Two men are required for the section a few yards further along,

so corkscrewed is it. These two call each other's attention from the conversations in the taverns by means of whistles, and wave red or green discs to each other and to the traffic, according to the unseen dangers or perhaps their whims. At night it is even more exciting and haphazard. The man by the interlaced corner has coloured lights to control his traffic, but as he is dozing on his stool and sets the light green for the oncoming tram only at the last second, it is doubtful whether anything coming the other way has time to stop at so sudden a red. As for the other corners, the men here do not even have lights, they merely gesticulate with their discs in almost total obscurity. The only bright lights are in the taverns.

The taverns of Lisbon are legion, and vary between fin-de-siecle palaces and basest dens. All the ones in this area are dens. The dens have sawdust on the floor for the customers to spit on to, spitting being a very popular habit among the lower orders in Portugal. Red wine is served straight from vast barrels kept behind the counter. This, with trams screaming past the door only a few feet away, is a most agreeable way to drink red wine. The red wine is probably not on any connoisseur's list, but I know of none better.

I do not know what you do if you want to spit on the floor of the Edwardian marble halls. They are in the smart quarters in the bottom of the Marquis of Pombal's city, particularly round the square of Rossio. The trams have gone from Rossio since the arrival of the Metro, but it is served by numerous buses, most of them AECs and Daimlers, looking very British except for having their doors — and, in the case of half-cabs, their cabs — on the wrong side.

Rossio, though an elegant square, is much disfigured by being a gathering place for undesirables. A great black man asks me, in English, if I want 'grass'. I certainly do not want 'grass', and retreat hastily. Rossio is also much disfigured by politics. Lisbon is possibly the most beautiful city in Europe, but its inhabitants delight, at least at the time of my visit in 1976, to spoil it by plastering every wall and monument with communist posters and similar evil spray-canned red exhortations.

The streets round Rossio are laid out at right angles, according to the good Marquis' plan, and each street, also according to his plan, is supposed to be given over to a particular trade. I must say that the trams coming down from Graça pass a whole row of shops selling nothing but buttons, and I cannot believe that all these shops can flourish in competition until I see them all full of customers.

At the lowest end of these streets, facing a noble expanse of the Tagus, is the great square of Comercio. One cannot suppose that the Marquis would approve

Above: A constant kaleidoscope of trams in the square of Comercio.

Top right: The tram track makes an inverted V at the summit of the line from Martim Moniz to Sao Tome. *Right:* The night in Lisbon. A 1905 tram with lights glowing in its original clerestory roof.

its being misused as a vast and hideously gleaming car park. He might even dislike the trams, though they stay fairly unobtrusively on its fringes. It is the terminus for several routes, and several more routes pass through it, so it is constantly alive with a wonderous kaleidoscope of tramcar movements, trams approaching and passing and veering over points and departing, always travelling in their same few directions yet never quite repeating the pattern of their motions. I spend many happy hours here just sitting under a brilliant sun in a bright blue sky watching these immaculate yellow trams, or in a warm darkness looking at the lights glowing from the clerestories.

Many of the lines which start from or pass through Comercio run along the banks of the Tagus, with no heavy gradients, and are served by bogie cars. While the four-wheel cars which climb the hills are, many of them, of traditional appearance, they are not in fact by

Lisbon standards very old, the oldest dating only from 1925. But some of the bogie cars are really ancient, being built in 1905-6, and if most of them are to a greater or lesser extent rebuilt, several of them retain clerestory roofs and an amazing aura of antiquity. There are few more entrancing sights than that of two or three of these gathered together in the Lisbon night.

Eastwards the bogie cars run to Poco do Bispo, along a road graced at one point by the Asylo de Dona Maria Pia and the convent buildings of Madre de Deus, and otherwise flanked by slums and some rather excellent ruined warehouses. The terminus boasts a Ladies' Convenience. So far as I can recall I have seen only two others in the whole of Lisbon.

Westwards, if you travel by tram as far as you can, to Cruz Quebrada, you have upwards of 10 km on a bogie car. Along this route, after visiting a splendid temple to Bacchus in Santo Amaro (south side of the

32

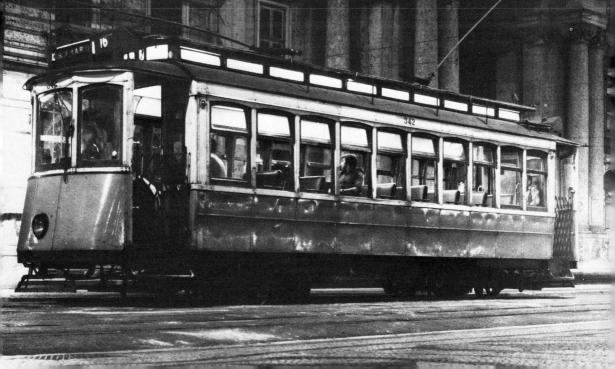

A delightful view from the bedroom. In the morning sun barrels of wine and crates of beer wait to be carried into a tavern. One of the newer trams and a trailer (only about 20 years old) sail past behind.

Right: Startling track and gradients in the Rua Vitor Cordon.

road east of the Ajuda junction), I wait for a tram in the shade of a corrugated tin roof supported by six poles. The next day I see this shelter lying collapsed on the pavement. Santo Amaro depot houses any number of dogs as well as a quantity of trams. Beyond is a broad pavement roofed by trees; here are shabby tarpaulined shelters, wooden benches, crude open fires and delicious smells. You may be able to eat very well at these impromptu restaurants, but I abstain on the grounds of their dubious cleanliness. Further west is Belem, with wonders well described in guidebooks, for which reason I refrain from description here, and also pass over the rest of the route, on the whole uneventful except for a pretty little tower at Alges; but I must

mention that when running for a tram at Alges I miss three bogie cars which pass in rapid succession and I board a fourth which comes immediately behind them and see a fifth which follows hard behind . . . certainly a delightful progression along the banks of the Tagus, five beautiful yellow bogie trams in line ahead.

From Comercio various of the bogie cars turn inland, through Pombal's city to the vast dusty square of Martim Moniz with its open market of stalls clad in sinister black canvas. Many of them play a weird Portuguese brand of pop music at immense volume; you can identify this length of tram track blindfold. Vegetable stalls have wondrously mishapen tomatoes. Old women shuffle in alarming black robes. Wild

34

young men, brown as berries, are more amiable than their villainious appearance suggests; they want me to send them some photographs, but, being illiterate, are unable to write their address. There are rows of bootblacks on the pavements. Like everywhere else in Lisbon, hundreds of people idle around doing nothing. Similarly, like everywhere else in Lisbon, numerous policemen idle around doing nothing. There are two sorts, some with blue and green kepis and some with flat grey caps, always armed with truncheons and pistols, and often smoking on duty. Naturally all imaginable types of beggar and cripple abound.

Beyond Martim Moniz the tramlines follow the Avenida Almirante Reis, which, unlike most of Lisbon, is probably the most dismal and ugly street in Iberia, although even here are some good pothouses. Actually, none of this north-east quarter has much charm.

The south-west is infinitely preferable. It has a network of tram routes with some unbelievable gradients and intricacies of trackwork, most noteworthy among them being a continuation of the line from Graça up the Calçada de Sao Francisco and the Rua Vitor Cordon. The terminus of Carmo has a Parisian charm with pigeons and gracious trees; a drunk argues with a tram crew and tries to board, they shut the iron grille in his face and start off, leaving him to some small boys who throw pebbles at him. At Estrela a constant and excellent string of trams comes and goes in front of the great basilica. By the junction at Rato — with more pretty trees — is one of the finest taverns in Lisbon, housing a noble tiled and marble altar in praise of wine, and cherubs supporting lamps. I am harangued at great length by a drinker, on what subject I know not, except that he shows me a socialist badge on his lapel and then turns the lapel over to reveal a communist badge.

This south-western district is one of the few where pretty maidens are to be seen in any quantity, and even then they are mostly something between 12 and 15 with a grace of youth which, it seems, soon vanishes. I must say, however, that when riding in the dusk on the back platform of 339, one of the original clerestories, somewhere near Santa Apolonia, I saw standing at a car stop a rapturously beautiful girl. Her features were definitely Portuguese yet much more soft and delicate than is usual, she was very slim, with bare brown legs and arms and a blue gingham dress which appeared almost transparent. But perhaps it was only the haze of red wine and the aura of 1906 tram which made her seem in that fleeting glimpse so marvellous. Anyway, I am not in Lisbon for maidens, however bewitching. Maidens elsewhere make trouble enough. I stay faithful to my bewitching red wine and my rapturously beautiful yellow trams.

Looking Back at Tracky

Photographs by G. H. F. ATKINS

A rear view of Barnsley bus station as it was in 1950, taken from the former Court House railway station. Many buses from the fleet of 'Tracky' — Yorkshire Traction — are in evidence.

A smart Yorkshire Traction Daimler CP6 of 1933, one of six fitted with Brush 28-seat bodies. It is seen in Nottingham in 1934.

Another 1933 delivery was this 20-seat Roe-bodied Leyland Cub, one of eight. It is seen at Skegness in 1935.

Leylands have always been popular at Barnsley, and this 1934 Leyland Lion LT5A with 32-seat Roe bus body was photographed at Doncaster Races in 1935.

The first of several batches of Leyland Tiger TS7s were Weymann 32-seat buses like 471, seen here at Southgate Street, Leicester in 1935.

There were 38 of these stylish Roe-
bodied Leyland Tiger TS7 32-seat
coaches delivered to Tracky in 1936; 549
is seen at Barnsley when new.

Six Leyland Titan TD5s were delivered in
1940, with Eastern Coach Works 54-seat
bodies, as seen at Barnsley in 1953.

Above: Tracky's new vehicle intake in the war years consisted almost entirely of utility Guy Arabs; only four had Northern Counties bodies, like 719, seen in 1954 at Barnsley depot. *Below:* At Dewsbury when new, a 1950 all-Leyland Titan PD2/1 56-seater.

Yorkshire Traction's first underfloor-engined buses were 20 Leyland Royal Tiger PSU1/9s delivered in 1951 and 43-seat Brush bodies; 911 is seen at Barnsley shortly after delivery.

A 1958 Leyland Tiger PSUC1/1 with 44-seat Park Royal body seen at Barnsley in August of the same year. In the background is one of Sheffield's unique ECW-bodied Leyland PD2s.

Barnsley again, and a 1967 view of a 1962 Leyland Titan PD3A/1 with Northern Counties 73-seat forward entrance body.

A victim of a terrorist bomb attack in 1970, an Ulsterbus Leyland PD2/10C with UTA/MCW body.

In 1965 the Government then in power in Northern Ireland decided in its wisdom to break up the loss-making Ulster Transport Authority into separate functional undertakings to operate road passenger services, railway passenger services and road freight services. This eventually led to the formation of Ulsterbus Ltd, a wholly-owned subsidiary of the Northern Ireland Transport Holding Company, which on 17 April 1967 took over the running of the road passenger services of the former UTA. There were of course some exceptions, these being in the Craigavon area, where a number of local services were operated by an independent concern — Sureline Coaches Ltd of Lurgan and in the North Antrim area, where two former UTA routes were run by another independent — Coastal Bus Services of Portrush; Coastal unfortunately succumbed to adverse economic conditions and was absorbed by Ulsterbus in April 1974. In Belfast, the city services, never part of UTA, were at that time still operated by Belfast Corporation Transport (later to become Citybus Ltd in April 1973, as another subsidiary of the Northern Ireland Transport Holding Company).

Ulsterbus has been in existence since 1966, and has bravely faced a host of unusual problems. R. C. LUDGATE recalls the undertaking's first 12 years.

Development and Determination

Over the past 12 years Ulsterbus has been very active in the development of express coach services covering local, cross-border and cross-channel operations. Other highly successful ventures include the development of luxury coach touring holidays in Britain, in addition to the already well-established Irish tours. The company operated its first seven-day Scottish tour in 1968, which was an immediate success and led to the build up of a tours programme covering many parts of Great Britain in its itineraries. But by far the most important development occurred on 29 November 1976, when the company became completely one-man operated in all its services.

Geographically the company's operations are divided into four areas — Central, Southern, Northern and Western, each under the control of an area manager. There are 19 main depots, each controlled by a depot manager, who is responsible to an area manager for all traffic operations including a number of sub-depots in his area. In addition to its extensive private hire work, Ulsterbus operates coach tours during the summer season and day excursions by bus from Belfast and other centres throughout the province.

Ulsterbus operates a network of bus and coach services covering some 2,760 bus route miles in the developing areas around Belfast and throughout the province with a fleet of some 930 buses and coaches and a staff of over 2,000. It carries over 64 million passengers per annum on

41

One of a number of Leyland Titan PD3/4s with UTA/MCW bodies used by the driving school for driver training. None of this type now remains in public service.

Right: Leyland Atlantean PDR2/1 with Alexander (Belfast) 85-seat body.

rural bus services, trunk services between Belfast and all provincial towns, city services in Londonderry and extensive town services in such places as Larne, Bangor and Craigavon. Belfast is linked to the growth towns in the south and west of the province by express services using the M1 motorway and, in the north, by the M2 motorway. The company also operates cross-border express coach services throughout the year between Dublin and Londonderry, Omagh, Dungannon, Magherafelt and Coleraine. A Belfast-Galway express service also operates all the year round and during the summer season provides connections to certain points in the west of Ireland.

Double deckers comprised 158 Leyland PD2/10Cs which were originally built by UTA between 1956-58; the bodies were of UTA/MCW construction and mounted on chassis rebuilt by UTA using running units from former Leyland PS2 single-deckers introduced in 1949, most of whose bodies were scrapped. This was done at the Duncrue Street Works.

There were also 132 Leyland PD3/4s with UTA/MCW bodies, including four with 64-seat bodies for use on airport services, the boot having been enlarged to provide more luggage space; and there were 36 Leyland PD2/1s with UTA 53-seat and 59-seat bodies.

Reverting once more to single-deckers there were 61 Leyland Royal Tigers with UTA B42F bodies. In addition there were several oddities: a Leyland Royal Tiger with Burlingham Seagull C41C body and two with Saro B44F bodies — all three vehicles came from Erne Bus Co, Enniskillen. Other buses not yet mentioned were three Leyland PS1s together with one Leyland PS2 — this was the only bus of the PS1 or PS2 type to be repainted in Ulsterbus livery and is happily preserved by a member of the Irish Transport Trust. Another odd-man out was the experimental Bedford VAL with 56-seat body built by UTA in 1964. Often referred to by the staff as the 'Torrey Canyon', it met with an untimely end when hijacked by terrorists near Strabane in 1973.

In 1966 in preparation for the

new company's formation the Ulsterbus management acquired a batch of secondhand 44-seat buses from Ribble which comprised 38 Leyland Royal Tigers with Leyland bodies and seven Leyland/MCW Olympics. The following year 48 secondhand Leyland Tiger Cub PSUC 1/3 Weymanns were acquired from Edinburgh Corporation. One of these, 9313, was the first bus to be painted in the new Ulsterbus livery of Riviera Blue/Trader Ivory with the fleetname in large letters on both sides. This later gave way to a fleetname using a smaller size letter, coupled with a name motif carried on the waistband, which became standard practice for all vehicles. These were followed later by 15 secondhand Leyland Leopard L1s from Western SMT with 30 seats and toilets, as specified for the Glasgow/London service. In the following years alterations were made to the seating of this batch together with eventual removal of the toilets and most subsequently worked as 41-seaters. In addition Ulsterbus assumed responsibility for all other remaining

UTA buses, irrespective of whether they were taxed or serviceable — there were 167 Leyland PS1s of which 50 were taxed; 30 Leyland PS2s of which only seven were taxed and 12 Leyland PD1s of which only one was taxed. Some of those taxed may have been operated in service when the company took over, but by the end of 1967 all had been withdrawn.

Cross-channel express coach services link Belfast with Glasgow/Edinburgh; north-east England; Scarborough/Filey; Preston/Manchester/Leeds and Blackpool. The only all year round service is Belfast-London via Birmingham; Londonderry is also linked with Glasgow and London. The cross-channel services are generally jointly operated with National Travel and Western SMT, but the Scarborough/Filey service is operated solely by Ulsterbus, whilst on the Blackpool service Western SMT coaches operate on charter hire. All these services use either the Larne-Stranraer or Cairnryan ferry sailings. The summer of 1978 saw the introduction of Interlink-Ireland

— a joint service operated by Ulsterbus Express and CIE Expressway linking Belfast and Londonderry with Athlone-Limerick/Cork/Wexford, thus making possible one of the longest coach journeys in Ireland.

Ulsterbus commenced operations with a fleet of 1,045 buses, comprising 699 single-deckers and 346 double-deckers of various makes. There were Austin 11- and 20-seaters; seven Bedford VASs; a Bedford SB5 with Duple body which was the prototype for the 74 school-buses which followed; further Bedford SBs had Duple Bella Vega bodies. Albions were represented by the Aberdonian MR11 with UTA DP41F bodies; the prototype of this batch was an Alexander-bodied demonstrator that had been acquired by UTA in 1960. AEC Reliances included a batch of 30 equipped with special low ratio axles for use on the hilly routes of the Londonderry City Services. A single vehicle from a different stable was a Commer TS3 with Beadle 43-seat body. There was a Saro-bodied Leyland Tiger Cub, the prototype for

a batch of 119 Leyland Tiger Cub PSUC1/5s — with UTA bus bodies; another batch of Tiger Cubs had UTA coach bodies. In addition there were six 36-seat Plaxton-bodied AEC Reliance coaches.

Mention must also be made of the six 'Wolfhound' express coaches built during 1965/66 by UTA on Leyland Leopard chassis. The exterior was finished in an unusual livery of grey and white with maroon flash, plus the word 'Wolfhound' in large letters and an illustration of an Irish Wolfhound dog carried on the bodysides.

The first new buses to be purchased by Ulsterbus were 70 Bedford VAM 14s with Duple 45-seat dual-purpose bodies (save 9208/64 which had Willowbrook bodies). The first to be delivered was 9203 in April 1967 which appeared in the new livery.

Early 1967 saw delivery of seven new Leyland Leopard PSU3/3 express coaches with 44-seat bodies built to Alexander Y type design by Potter of Belfast Ltd. Delivered the same year were six Plaxton-bodied 41-seat Leyland Leopard PSU4/3

coaches.

From then on Ulsterbus embarked on a big programme of fleet rejuvenation and new deliveries, which over the years gradually displaced many of the older buses. The first major order in 1968 was for 75 vehicles comprising 10 Bristol LHs, five Leyland Leopard express coaches, 40 Leyland Leopards and 20 Bristol RELLs.

The first new vehicles to be delivered were the Bristol LH6Ls with Potter dual-pupose 41-seat bodies. Next came five Leyland Leopard PSU3A/4R express coaches with Potter 49-seat bodies, except 495 which had 47 seats to provide extra luggage space. The period 1968/69 saw delivery of the first of the now ubiquitous Leyland Leopard 36ft long vehicles, which largely dominate the fleet, this was a batch of 20 PSU3A/4Rs with Potter 53-seat bodies, followed by another 30 which were dual purpose 49-seaters; the last batch had Alexander (Belfast) bodies and were intended for use on airport services.

Here your author must digress for a moment to explain to the reader about the change of name in regard to the local bodybuilder. MH Coachworks (formerly MH Cars Ltd of Dunmore, Belfast), came into being in 1961, and in 1965 the company changed its name to Potters of Belfast Ltd (same address). This however, was purely a change of name for in 1969, the wellknown Scottish firm of Walter Alexander & Co (Coachbuilders) Ltd of Falkirk, purchased a majority shareholding in Potter and thus the firm of Walter Alexander & Co (Belfast) Ltd came into being using the same premises until in April 1973 when it moved to larger premises at Mallusk, Co Antrim, where all bodybuilding is now carried out.

It should be noted that Ulsterbus did not continue the tradition of its predecessors in building its own bus bodies. For three years before the take-over there had been close collaboration between the companies, however; Potters had built bodies on behalf of the Falkirk works and exchange of design

material, fibreglass moulds, etc had taken place. The Ulsterbus standard body contained many common design features with the Falkirk firm's Y type body.

New and larger buses were now urgently required for the Londonderry city services and in 1969 delivery was taken of 20 Leyland-engined Bristol RELLs, with bodywork to Potters design, which because of production limitations were built by Alexanders at Falkirk, and had dual-entrance 44-seat bodies. The selection of this model followed tests with demonstration buses including an ECW-bodied Bristol RELL (LAE 770E) and a Marshall-bodied AEC Swift (LYY 872D). The Swift became Coastal No 6 and was re-registered with the Co Antrim marque CIA 3000; it ultimately returned to the Ulsterbus fleet in 1974 when Coastal was taken over.

Then followed one of the largest orders ever placed by Ulsterbus, for 300 new buses for delivery during 1970/71; this comprised 20 Leyland Leopard express coaches, 240 Leyland Leopard buses and 40 Leyland Atlantean double-deckers. The first to be delivered were 10 express coaches which were Leyland Leopard PSU3A/4Rs and 10 which were PSU3/4Rs — all had Alexander (Belfast) 49-seat bodies. During the same period another 150 Leopards were delivered, all with Alexander (Belfast) bodies to either 49-seat dual purpose or 53-seat stage carriage design.

Leaving new vehicles aside for the moment, it should be noted that there were two secondhand additions to the fleet. In 1970 a Leyland Tiger Cub was acquired from the 6th Sea Scout Group, Newtownards (originally ex-Edinburgh Corporation), and in 1971 a Willowbrook-bodied Ford R192 (CNO 797G), an ex-Ford demonstrator was purchased; this was later withdrawn and sold to Cassidy of Scotstown, Eire, but was destroyed in a bomb attack on Lisburn Depot before he had taken delivery.

In 1971 six 49-seat Plaxton/Leopard coaches were delivered — these were intended for

Left: A Bedford YLQ with Alexander (Belfast) 45-seat bus body on local service in the Coleraine area.

An express coach with Alexander (Belfast) 49-seat body on Leyland Leopard PSU3B/4R chassis.

extended tour work. During 1972/73, 40 new Leyland Atlantean PDR2/1s were delivered with Alexander (Belfast) bodies. In 1972 another 90 Leopard 53-seat buses went into service.

An unusual purchase in 1973 was a Leyland National demonstrator, which became No 1600 (EOI 8060) — this is the only one in the fleet and indeed in the whole of Ireland. The same year saw delivery of 100 Bristol LH6Ls with Alexander (Belfast) 45-seat bodies. In 1974 two different batches of Bedfords were ordered, 100 YRQs and 25 YRTs. Of these, two YRQs had Duple Dominant 41-seat coach bodies and the other 98 had Alexander (Belfast) 45-seat bus bodies. Similar 53-seat Alexander bodies were fitted to the YRTs. 1976 saw delivery of more new Bedfords, this time YLQs — two with Duple Dominant 41-seat coach bodies, and 48 with Alexander (Belfast) 45-seat bus bodies. Purchase of lightweight chassis for bus operation ceased after delivery of the YLQs.

More Leyland Leopards were delivered during 1974/75 in several batches — 31 with Alexander (Belfast) 49-seat dual-purpose bodies, and four received Duple Dominant 49-seat coach bodies. In 1976 30 Leopards were delivered also fitted with Alexander (Belfast) 49-seat dual-purpose bodywork. Two batches delivered in 1977 totalled a further 30, most with Alexander (Belfast) 49-seat bodies, with the exception of six which had Duple Dominant II 49-seat bodywork.

Based on operational experience gained with previous Bristol RELL/Alexander vehicles on Londonderry city services, it was decided that new city and suburban buses should be of this type and incorporate many improved features. During the period 1975-78 some 170 of these buses were delivered to Ulsterbus, many almost identical vehicles being delivered also to Citybus.

The Bristol chassis are fitted with Gardner engines and the bodies, which are of aluminium alloy construction, are built by Alexander (Belfast). A batch of 40 was delivered in 1975, 28 with 44-seat dual entrance bodies and 12 with 50-seat bodies. Another 15 dual entrance buses were delivered in 1976, and during 1977/8, a further 115 buses were put into traffic. Also during 1978 another 50 Leopards were delivered; four have Duple Dominant I 53-seat bodies for express services while the rest have Alexander dual-purpose 49-seat bodies. A further ten Leyland Leopard PSU3E/4Rs — four touring coaches with Duple Dominant II and six express coaches with Dominant I bodies arrived during 1979, followed by 50 similar vehicles but fitted with the more conventional Alexander dual-purpose body.

In January 1978 a Bedford YLQ with Duple Dominant II 45-seat luxury coach body was bought from SMT Sales and Service Ltd, Glasgow. This replaced a Bedford YRQ/Duple Dominant 41-seater coach, which had been earlier maliciously destroyed. The same year, seven ex-Grey-Green Coaches were added to the fleet, these being Leyland Leopard PSU3B/4Rs with Plaxton Panorama Elite bodies. They were painted in express livery and one is a 12-metre coach, the first of its kind in the fleet. Two other smaller second-hand coaches, both 29-seaters, were also added to the fleet — a Bedford VAS5/Duple Vista 25, came via SMT, Glasgow and was originally registered TPT 445K; and another VAS but with Baby Dominant bodywork was acquired from Wetherdair Ltd, Ballywalter, Co Down, in October 1977.

Other used vehicles to enter the fleet included ex-London Transport AEC Merlins consisting of 17 MB types and five dual entrance MBA types, all with MCW bodywork. During 1977/78, 14 Potter-bodied Daimler Fleetline double-deckers and three Leyland Atlanteans with bodies by MH Cars were transferred from the Citybus fleet, mainly replacing life-expired Leyland PD3/4s, which are now very few in number. By late 1979, it was expected that most of the former UTA vehicles will have gone.

Demonstrators were many in the early years and one very interesting vehicle worthy of mention (if only for the fact that Ulsterbus was the only operator in the United Kingdom to test it) was a Swedish Scania-Vabis C70 'Capitol' single-decker from the Stockholm municipal undertaking, which was operated on the Londonderry city services. A number of modifications had to be made before the Northern Ireland PSV Authorities were prepared to grant special dispensation for the bus to be used for a short experimental period during which it was temporarily re-registered with Belfast marque 920 TZ.

A Ford demonstrator which arrived early in 1970 was the unique Willowbrook/Ford R192 KEV 953J with semi-automatic transmission, which became No 3 in the fleet during its stay: it was later returned after some two months evaluation. This bus also appeared at the Earls Court Show that year in Ulsterbus livery. Another demonstrator to appear in 1970 was Metro-Scania single-deck integral bus VWD 451H which was operated over a wide variety of routes before being returned some five weeks later. One other demonstrator not yet mentioned was Seddon Pennine RU KWW 901K which arrived early in 1971 for evaluation. Of the aforementioned demonstrators, none of these types was ever introduced into the Ulsterbus fleet.

Another interesting event in the history of Ulsterbus still be be recorded was in late 1967 when 50 ex-UTA Leyland PS1s/PS2s were hired to CIE to alleviate its acute shortage of buses for school duties. These ran for about two years before being withdrawn and were later scrapped by the Hammond Lane Foundry Co, Dublin, except PS1 8570 which passed to the TMSI Dublin for preservation. In 1971 10 Bedford SB/Duple Bella Vega coaches were also loaned to CIE for a period of time, but these were all later returned to Ulsterbus.

The last Leyland PD2/10C double-deckers ran on 30 December 1972 and on that date only four remained in service; these 60-seat double-deckers were the last public service buses in the Ulsterbus fleet with half-cabs, exposed radiators and rear entrances.

Formerly London Transport MB360, this AEC Merlin/MCW was the first to appear in Ulsterbus livery.

To alleviate a shortage of vehicles due to late delivery of new Leyland Atlanteans to Citybus in 1975, 14 Leyland Leopards were loaned by Ulsterbus, and most were returned in November. At the same time two Leyland PD3/4s were also loaned for school duties; after a period of time, these were withdrawn and sold for scrap. In addition many of the ex-Edinburgh Corporation Leyland Tiger Cubs were transferred to the Citybus fleet, being used mainly on school duties and also for a short period on the Citylink service. All these buses ran in Ulsterbus colours but with the Citybus fleetname.

By early 1978 only two of the large class of Leyland Tiger Cub PSUC1/5s remained in service but were later detaxed and put into the Reserve Fleet. Of the two others remaining on the active list, 348 was in use by the Driving School in Belfast, whilst 309 was retired to the Reserve Fleet, having been used as a Staff Bus until replaced by a PD3/4 double-decker early in 1979.

Mid-1978 saw the withdrawal of a number of the ex-Western SMT Leyland Leopard L1s which were being converted for use as tow-cars, thus displacing the former ex-Ribble Royal Tigers from similar work. One point of interest to record is that by early 1979, there was still one ex-UTA Leyland PS1 (No 8517), in use as a tow-car at Armagh depot, this being the only survivor of its type.

An important facet of Ulsterbus operations is the well-established driver training school, with its headquarters located at Oxford Street depot, Belfast, together with a smaller training school at Londonderry. In earlier years Leyland Titan PD2/10s, with crash change boxes were used for driver training, but these have been superseded by Leyland PD3/4s with crash/synchromesh gear-boxes. Nine such vehicles are used for instructional purposes in Belfast and two in Londonderry.

Since the political unrest and civil disturbances, which have dominated life in the Province since August 1969, Ulsterbus has lost over 380 buses valued at about £15 million, but despite all the arson and bomb attacks on depots etc, which have been repeatedly occurring, the company has remained consistently profitable for the past 10 years. The company's financial results are believed to be the envy of many cross-channel and European bus companies who are struggling to get out of the red.

As an example of the troubles faced by Ulsterbus, in the first six months of 1978, three separate bomb attacks were made on depots in Londonderry (Pennyburn) (where 23 buses were destroyed and 17 damaged); in Belfast (Smithfield) where the depot was completely destroyed in addition to 21 buses and at Newry where seven buses were lost.

Epsom Assaults. An East Kent open-top Guy Arab III with
Levingtons of Brentwood, painted in Jubilee livery, adds a royal
touch to Epsom racecourse in June 1978.

Poles Apart

London's last trolleybus ran in 1962, and MICHAEL DRYHURST fondly remembers the conversion programme, the vehicles and the routes.

Left: At Manor House, Weymann-bodied J1 AEC 945 stands next to MCCW-bodied H1 Leyland 762.

After deliveries of short-wheelbase Leylands came 250 AEC 664T trolleybuses which with different bodybuilders broke down in the C1/C2/C3 classes. A number of vehicles within each class was fitted with part-enclosed rear wheels (spats), such as seen here on C3 303 at Stanmore Circus.

One of the depressing, nay boring, things about getting older is the way that the once-familiar becomes the oft-remembered. And, seemingly, overnight. And in many cases these once-familiar adjuncts of one's life disappear without trace.

Picture Post ... Variety theatres ... Lyons Tea Shops ... proper money (you know pennies, ha'pennies, threepenney bits, sixpences, halfcrowns) ... politeness ... Timothy Whites ... Sunday postal collections ... and trolleybuses. Especially London trolleybuses.

Such is the rapidity of the passage of time that I find it incredible that the conversion of the London trolleybus system to motorbus operation started in earnest over 20 years ago, in March 1959, and this feeling of dismay at how long ago it was is heightened by the fact that there are still many parts of London that I associate with trolleybuses, and I find it extremely hard to reconcile the fact that they have long since gone; in a similar way, it was years before I got used to the Embankment without trams. There are still some reminders of London Transport trolleybuses evident in the streets of the capital — electrical boxes at certain road junctions, or traction poles still in use

as street-lighting standards — but these apart, the uninitiated would not be aware of their having happened.

Because the time between the announcement of the abandonment of the London trolleybus system and the actual implementation of the conversion programme was some five years, one felt that the dreaded day would not actually dawn, and that fate would invent some sort of last-minute reprieve. Many felt that this had arrived with the Anglo-French invasion of the Suez Canal area in 1956, which resulted in a period of petrol rationing and put trolleybuses in the limelight once again. But diplomacy won the day, the oil flowed again, and the fate of the trolleybuses was sealed.

But then, the writing had been on the wall for some time. World War II had interrupted the tram conversion programme of the London Passenger Transport Board, the last such conversion having taken place in June 1940 when the Commercial Road and Mile End Road routes went over to trolleybuses. This had left but three North London tram routes to be converted, and when LPTB chairman Lord Latham announced the postwar resumption of the tram conversion scheme it was noted that the replacing

49

vehicles were to be motorbuses, and his speech at that time suggested that the trolleybus system was not to be regarded as a permanent feature of the London scene.

When one considers the way in which the previously-converted tram routes had become trolleybus routes virtually on a one-for-one basis, instead of extending the new trolleybus routes to open up links (such as along Marylebone Road to Tottenham Court Road, or from Canons Park to Stanmore Station, etc), one must seriously question if the overlords of 55 Broadway always intended the trolleybus to be a passing panacea to replace worn-out rolling stock whilst still utilising equipment that was good for many more years (equipment that had required initial high-capital investment) and to use that equipment until it was spent, by which time it would have shown a return on its original investment?

But back to the system itself. A number of routes was withdrawn during the life of the system, mostly as a result of service cuts, but the first actual conversion of a trolleybus route to motorbus operation was with the resumption of the tram conversion programme, when with Stage 1 in October 1950 the

trams at Wandsworth depot were ousted, and it became WD bus garage. However, Wandsworth had a small allocation of trolleybuses for route 612, which ran from the Princes Head, Battersea, to Mitcham. In a way it was poetic justice, insomuch as the 612 had replaced the suburban end of the 12 tram; and now the remainder of the 12, from Clapham to London Bridge, was being replaced by the 44 bus, which was being projected over the 612 to restore the link severed by the trolleybus route. Wandsworth also had some night workings on the 628, and these, together with Wandsworth's D3-type Leyland trolleybuses, were transferred to Hammersmith depot.

The trolleybuses and trams had hitherto been a seperate operating entity within the LTE, but with the run-down of the trams the trolleybuses became part of Central Buses, the most obvious effect of this being the allocation of depot codes and their appearance on the trolleybuses themselves, only a running number having been carried previously.

In 1954 it was announced that, as and when they became due for replacement, the London trolleybuses were to be replaced by a 'revolutionary' new type of motorbus, designed by ACV and LTE, to be known as

Left: The last member of the BRCW-bodied J3 class acted as the prototype for the 90 N1, and J3 1054 is seen here at Finsbury Square, Moorgate, next to standard all-Leyland K1 1210.

N1 1587A stands in Minories bus station, surrounded by N1 and F1 trolleybuses and RTW motorbuses. 1587 was one of two N1s which were victims of bomb damage and were subsequently rebodied, in this case by Weymann.

the Routemaster. (ACV was the parent selling organisation of AEC and Park Royal.) At the same time as this announcement was made, orders were placed for 850 Routemasters, for trolleybus replacements.

But despite the threat of extinction, the London trolleybus system continued to thrive, as if immortal. Vehicles were regularly overhauled and repainted at Fulwell Works, route revisions took place, including the occasional extension (over existing track), and drivers continued to be trained for trolleybuses. In fact, I saw a trolleybus with 'L' plates training out of Isleworth Depot in February 1962, when there was only three months of trolleybus operation left. Although, by now, part of the Central Bus Division, the trolleybus system retained most of its distinctive features.

Although red oxide paint was being daubed on the wheel rings of the motorbuses, the trolleybuses retained their chromed wheel rings (AECs) or aluminium ones (Leylands). The cream relief on the buses had been whittled down to the cantrail band between decks, but the trolleybuses still had their two cream bands, lined out in black, together with a red

front dome, red-oxide roof and brown rear dome. The roof had originally been silver, but as an air raid precaution this was replaced by red-oxide. The trolleybuses also carried a blue and gold trolleybus motif on the front panel and rear window. The interiors of London trolleybuses really bore no resemblance to their motorbus counterparts, as many of the electric vehicles had blue interiors, and although many of these were subsequently repainted into the more usual brown and cream interior livery, many of the blues survived to the end. And then there were the coin testers, little chrome fittings with a number of grooves inset, these grooves being the width of the then coins of the realm. Every trolleybus had one on each deck, but in 15 years of concentrated riding on London trolleybuses, I never saw them ever used. Maybe the conductors did not know what they were anyway? Earlier trolleybuses had bench seats alongside the driver within the full front, but these were subsequently removed and the front bulkhead became a full-width fitting.

The vehicles were classified into lettered classes, and then sub-divided with a number suffix, which usually covered a variation of bodywork or electrical equipment. The standard London trolleybus was a 30ft long, 7ft 6in wide three-axle chassis, on which was mounted a 70-seat (H30/40R) body built by a number of manufacturers, whilst the chassis were by AEC and Leyland. To the layman, the London trolleybus types were virtually the same, but in fact each class had features which made it readily distinguishable.

The A1 and A2 classes, trolleybuses 1-60, were 1931 AEC 663T vehicles, with Union Construction Co H56R bodies, to a style that was a mixture of LGOC LT-type bus, and UCC 'Feltham' type tram. London United (both LUT and UCC were underground Group subsidiaries) had introduced these trolleybuses to the south-west suburbs of London, when it converted a number of tram routes in the Kingston and Twickenham areas in 1931. With the formation of the London Passenger Transport Board in July 1933 the new organisation was quick to implement a programme of trolleybuses for trams, and between 1935 and 1940 virtually all of the north London tram routes were converted to trolleybus operation, together with pockets in south-east and south-west London. During this period over 1,600 trolleybuses were delivered, which gave London Transport the largest fleet of such vehicles in the world.

The first bulk delivery to the Board were really non-standard vehicles. These were short-wheelbase three-axle trolleybuses, the short length being felt desirable for hilly routes such as Anerley Hill and Highgate Hill, the vehicles being fitted with run back brakes and bodies by Birmingham Railway Carriage and Wagon Co, or Brush, with accommodation for 60 seated passengers. The same year (1935) saw the first large order for AECs, 50 30ft long 664T chassis with Metropolitan Cammell Carriage & Wagon Co and Weymann bodies, followed by a further 200 AEC 664T in 1936, which were also bodied by BRCW and MCCW, this group being the C1/C2/C3 classes. The Ds were Leylands, D1 being a one-off job, the next 100 being 69-seat D2s (MCCW) and 70-seat D3s (BRCW). The E1/E2/E3 'century' had bodies by Brush (554-603, with a very distinctive front dome), MCCW (604-628) and Park Royal. The first of over 400 Leyland trolleybus bodies arrived with the F1 class in 1937, followed by a solitary experimental AEC numbered 754. The next batch was another 150 Leylands, this being the MCCW-bodied H1 class; the letter G was never used. Next came 47 AECs with Weymann bodies and the final and 48th member (952) of the J1 class had a MCCW body of the H1 type. 953 was a prototype chassisless L1 with a handsome Weymann body, whilst 954 was the prototype chassisless L2, an MCCW body with AEC running units, unique in the fleet in being the only trolleybus

built for London to have the cream relief continued under the windscreen. The J2 and J3 were another 100 BRCW-bodied AECs, the last (1054) having a body vastly different from the rest, being the prototype for the N1 class.

Next came 300 all-Leyland trolleybuses, types K1 and K2 covering stock numbers 1055-1354. Twenty-four MCCW chassisless machines with AEC units came next, these being the L1 (1355-69) L2 (1370-8) and X5 (1379), the last-mentioned being especially interesting in that it had rear offside doors to the platform, for use at the island stations in the Kingsway tram subway. As far as is known 1379 only made one trip through the subway, under battery power and without passengers. Further MCCW-AEC chassisless trolleybuses were the 150 L3 trolleybuses, which were to a more rounded design (together with the L1/2) than hitherto. Built on what was described as the 'unit Construction principle' were the 25 M1s, which had AEC running units married to a Weymann body. All of these London trolleybuses had half-drop opening windows, but some, like L3s 1527-9, had sliding ventilators, whilst M1 1532 had a mixture of both! The N-class comprised 115 AECs, of which the N1 was 1555-1644, and N2 1645-1669. These latter 25 trolleybuses had Park Royal bodies, and were not really like any of the other London classes, being the standard Park Royal body adopted to London practice. In 1940 Leyland supplied its last batch of bodies for the London fleet, when K3s 1672-1696 were delivered, followed by another 25 Leylands with MCCW bodies of the L3 style, PIs 1697-1721. These latter vehicles completed the prewar trolleybus deliveries to the LPTB.

Two vehicles not mentioned are 1670/1. The former was an AEC with a handsome English Electric body, which became an air raid casualty, whilst 1671 was unique in two respects. It had a Lancashire registration, having been a Leyland demonstrator (DTD 649) and a three-axle layout, but with a difference — it had two axles at the front, being a twin-steer machine in the style of a heavy lorry, and this vehicle survived until 1956.

A shortage of trolleybuses in the early part of the war led to the hiring of 18 Park Royal-bodied MS2 Sunbeams from Bournemouth Corporation which featured that operator's standard arrangement of a front exit and staircase, combined with the normal rear loading arrangement. In 1942 Metro-Cammell had finished bodying an order of 43 trolleybuses for two South African operators, there being 23 Leylands for Durban, and 20 AECs for Johannesburg. The action of enemy submarines was such that it was decided that these 8ft wide buses would be redirected to the LPTB, which put them into Ilford depot, releasing the hired

Although Park Royal supplied many London Transport bus and coach bodies, it produced very few trolleybus bodies. In 1940, 25 Park Royal-bodied AECs, class N2, were delivered — virtually standard provincial style bodies camouflaged for London use.

The last Leylands ordered by LPTB were the 25 P1 trolleybuses, which had Metro-Cammell bodies of the style associated with the L3 AECs. The P1s were always associated with Edmonton and Hammersmith depots, and the latter's 1700 is seen at Shepherd's Bush on the peak hour 626 route.

Another peak hour route was the 695 (Bow-Ilford), which fell victim of service cuts in November 1959. A month earlier it was being worked by SA2 1731, one of the Metro-Cammell-bodied Leylands that had been intended for use in Durban.

The final London trolleybus class was the Q1, combining a BUT 9641T chassis with MCCW 70-seat body, and 1777 is seen on a wet and windy day at Hampton Court.

Sunbeams and replacing war-damaged vehicles. These buses became the SA (for South Africa) class, 1722-31 being the SA1, 1732-46 the SA2 and 1747-64 the SA3. All of the buses had rear entrances and staircases, but were fitted with a sliding front exit behind the nearside cab, and the top half of the windows were fitted with tinted glass, for their intended area of operation.

After the war, AEC and Leyland pooled their trolleybus building resources, to form British United Traction, with AEC building double-deckers at Southall, and Leyland single-deckers in Lancashire.

In 1948 London Transport took delivery of 77 BUT 9641T chassis, with MCCW bodies, which was the standard London trolleybus, updated — an 8ft wide chassis with a more shapely body, (but showing its L3 lineage) of five-bay construction. In 1952, a further 50 BUTs were received, taking the same class denotion (Q1) as the previous 77. These buses completed the delivery of trolleybuses to London.

During the war, a number of LT trolleys was damaged by enemy action, and many of these were subsequently rebodied, by Weymann, East Lancs and Northern Coachbuilders Ltd, each vehicle receiving a suffix letter to its fleetnumber, these being respectively A, B or C according to the coachbuilder. Some of the

short-wheelbase Leylands received new bodies, being lengthened to 30ft in the process.

And so the inevitable took place — the first stage of the Buses for Trolleybuses conversion scheme, all of which took place on Tuesday nights/Wednesday mornings. The 3rd March 1959 was a dismal, wet day, with incessant rain, which virtually washed away the 654, 696 and 698, affecting Carshalton (CN) and Bexleyheath (BX) depots, and seeing the end of the short-wheelbase trolleybuses. During the previous year, in the summer of 1958, London Transport had suffered a crippling strike of bus crews, which lost them much traffic that was never subsequently re-couped, and one result was that a large portion of the existing motorbus fleet became surplus to the then current requirements. Therefore RT and RTL buses were used for the initial stages of the trolleybus conversion scheme, both BX and CN receiving RTs for Stage I, those at the latter garage being almost 100% of the top-box variety. Six weeks later, Stage II; 14 April, and more heavy rain, and the Leyland trolleybuses at Clapton and Lea Bridge came off, seeing the demise of the 555, 581 and 677. Lea Bridge was closed and operations were transferred to the nearby Leyton bus garage, although Lea Bridge remained in use as the terminus of certain 661

journeys, whilst Clapton received a complement of RTL buses for its replacement workings. Bow and Ilford were converted on a balmy summer evening in August 1959, which saw the end of the South African trolleybuses; however, these were put into store, as it was felt that their good condition might find them a buyer, but none was forthcoming and so they succumbed to the breakers yard. The George Cohen 600 Group obtained the contract for scrapping the London trolleybuses, and although a few were broken up at Charlton Works, the great majority was dealt with on land alongside Colindale depot, and as this was physically connected to the system, most trolleybuses were driven under their own power to the scrapyard. The Clapton and Lea Bridge K types from Stage II, and the Bow N1s from Stage III, were allocated to other depots in the system, where they replaced earlier trolleybuses that had gone for scrap.

Stage IV was in November 1959, when Poplar depot was converted, together with a few workings from West Ham. This conversion was auspicious in two ways — it was the first use of Routemaster buses in the trolleybus conversion, and also saw the first funeral ceremony, when the last trolleybus into the depot was accompanied by a procession of crews with flaming torches. Poplar's L3 trollies went to other

depots, replacing older vehicles. At the same time Clay Hall bus garage was closed and workings were transferred to Bow and Poplar, Athol Street, although the latter closed in 1961.

Walthamstow and West Ham depots featured in Stages V and V1 respectively, on 3 February and 27 April 1960. E2 class trolleybus 622 had inaugurated West Ham's trolleybus services in 1937, and became the last trolleybus into WH depot, 23 years later, being suitably decorated for the occasion. Both of these depots had been municipally-owned prior to the formation of the LPTB. Coincidental with Stage V1 was the closure of Forest Gate bus garage, operations being transferred to WH.

In July 1960, the 'fag-end' 611 Highgate Hill route was converted, together with all of Hammersmith depot workings, which saw the demise of the 626, 628 and 630. The British European Airways coach fleet, used on services between Central London and Heathrow and Northolt Airports, was moved into the former Hammersmith trolleybus depot. This Stage, VII, marked the halfway post of the programme.

The final conversion of 1960 was on 9 November when Stage VIII saw the withdrawal of trolleybuses from Hanwell; this depot worked two services, the 607 from Shepherds Bush to Uxbridge, and the circuitous

655, which in its full-length form, from Acton Vale to Clapham Junction was London's longest trolleybus route, 14.5 miles. By now, over 700 Routemasters had been delivered, whilst seven trolleybus classes had passed into history, and over half the trolleybus fleet had been scrapped.

The year 1961 saw the replacement of all the remaining North London trolleybus routes. On 1 February, Highgate lost the 513/613, 517/617, 615, 639 and 653, as a result of which many of the L3 trolleybuses became redundant, but most of them moved to south west London, where they replaced the postwar Q1 BUTs. As Fulwell and Isleworth depots were stocked with these postwar trolleybuses, and the presence of the works attached to Fulwell Depot meant that their area of operation was self-sustaining, it had been originally intended that the Q1s would be worked to the end of their economic lives, which was reckoned to be 1968, and so a pocket of trolleybus operation was to be kept until that time. However, during 1960/1 buyers for 125 of the postwar trolleybuses were found amongst a number of Spanish operators, and having thus lost the main reason for prolonging trolleybus operation until 1968, Stage XIV was moved forward six years, to May 1962.

But back to 1961: 26 April saw Highgate's last trolleybus operation, together with some Edmonton routes. Highgate had a Sunday allocation on the primarily Finchley-operated 609 route, and this continued after the demise of Highgate's trolleybuses, the replacement HT Sunday Routemasters carrying 609 blinds, this being the only instance of replacing buses carrying the trolleybus route number. Under the London Transport route numbering scheme, trolleybus routes carried numbers in the 500 and 600 series, usually with just the addition of a 5 or a 6 to the previous tram route number, and thus following the pattern whereby routes with even numbers were mostly south of the Thames, all odd route numbers being north of the river.

Edmonton finally lost its trolleybuses in July 1961, together with Stamford Hill, and in November inroads were made into Finchley, whilst Wood Green succumbed to the all-conquering bus. The RM workings on the 609 ceased, whilst 24 of the lengthened RMs (30ft long) were put into Finchley for use on the 609 replacement, the 104. These long Routemasters were originally to have been classified ER, but they entered service as RMLs, the prototype Routemaster with Leyland running units, RML3, becoming plain RM3. In addition the now-familiar upper-and lower-case intermediate destination blinds were introduced at this time.

The west London routes disappeared in sub-zero temperatures early in January 1962, when the 645,

A reminder of the original London United Tramways trolleybus services of 1931, preserved AEC 663T/UCC vehicle number 1 on the Kingston Loop during a special run on the last day of London's trolleybuses, 8 May 1962.

660, 662, and 666 came off, with Colindale being closed and Finchley and Stonebridge going over to bus operation. On the other side of London, the old Public bus garage, West Green, was closed, and operations were transferred to the former Wood Green trolleybus depot.

And so the final day came. It was a warm, early summer's day, 8 May 1962, and the routes working out of Fulwell and Isleworth were with trolleybuses full of enthusiasts. With its BUTs gone to Spain, the small Isleworth allocation for the 657 was with K type Leylands, L3 AECs being Fulwell's stock. During the afternoon, preserved A1 trolley No 1 was brought out of retirement, and did a run from Fulwell to Kingston and back, being followed by L3 1521, both buses being suitably inscribed for the occasion. 1521 subsequently went back into service, and was the last trolleybus to run into Fulwell depot, thus closing the system.

Fortunately, a number of London trolleybuses has been preserved, a recent addition to these ranks being the return of one of the Q1 BUTs, sold to Spain 18 years ago.

Roadliners in Retrospect

The rear-engined Daimler Roadliner model, never a totally successful chassis, is remembered in photographs by MARTIN J. PERRY

Above: Black & White was an important Roadliner customer between 1966 and 1970, and these coaches are from the last batch, with Perkins V8 engines and Plaxton Elite bodies. 318 is in Black & White colours, while 316 wears National white.

Potteries also bought Roadliners in fair numbers, but did not keep them for a full life. This former Potteries 1967 Roadliner/Plaxton bus is seen with Tartan Travel of Nantwich, alongside an ex-Black & White Roadliner coach.

Wolverhampton Corporation bought AEC Swifts and Daimler Roadliners in 1967, and perhaps surprisingly the Roadliners outlived the Swifts, into West Midlands PTE hands. 716 is seen at Bridgnorth in 1970, a Cummins V6-engined bus with Strachans body.

Ignoble end for a Daimler — one of Potteries 1967 batch of Plaxton-bodied Roadliners acting as a seasonal refreshment bar at Hylton Park service area on the M6 motorway in Staffordshire.

It is almost 18 years ago since the Bedford VAL14 made its debut at the 1962 Commercial Motor Show at Earls Court. Doubtless at the time there were many who viewed it with misgivings. 'A twin-steering single-decker? That won't catch on! Why it's been tried out before and found hardly any takers.'

Indeed that had been the case, a quarter of a century previously at a similar Show Leyland had exhibited its prototype TEP1 chassis (christened the Gnu by that zoologically-motivated firm): 30ft long, by law it had to have a third axle, but unlike current models of the Tiger, the Gnu's third axle had been positioned at the front of the chassis. Even the standard 8.6 litre diesel engine had been situated unorthodoxically *beside* the driver, whilst the radiator was located on the nearside at the front of the vehicle. Alexander had built a 40-seat body for it, with a front entrance 5ft ahead of the leading axle. WG 6608 joined the Alexanders fleet, along with a second Gnu the following year.

In 1938 Leyland had introduced its Steer trolleybus, based on twin-steering principles, but with the forwardmost axle much nearer to the front of the chassis than had been the case with the original Gnu. Then in 1939 an improved design Gnu (designated the TEC2) appeared with a chassis very like that of the Steer, thus necessitating the repositioning of the radiator at the front of the bus. The City Coach Company, which had purchased the third and last of the TEP1s, proceeded to take into its fleet all five of the TEC2s to see the light of day. In 1940 there appeared the one and only Leyland Panda, which was basically a Gnu with an underfloor 8.6 litre engine placed asymetrically against the right hand frame member, plus a drop frame extension, which enabled Alexander to fit a 45-seat central-entrance bus body on to WG 9519 in 1941.

The next step in the twin-steering story is really not a step at all, for in 1947 Leyland built two Tigers (designated PS2/10s) for the Northern Ireland Road Transport Board with 30ft×7ft 6in bodywork

The Bedford VAL six-wheel coach chassis was welcomed with amazement and scepticism. DAVID KAYE reviews its 10-year production run.

Six Wheels Come Full Circle

for use on the Aldergrove Airport route. The NIRTB built its own 27-seat central entrance half-decker bodies for this pair. Really the PS2/10 was an ordinary PS2 Tiger with a lengthened wheelbase of 18ft 9in and a second front axle. This latter was to be a temporary feature until the law was amended allowing two-axle buses to be 30ft long.

A solitary 8ft wide version (type PS2/11) entered service with City Coach with a 39-seat central-entrance single-deck body in 1949. This eventually ended up as a two-axle 69-seat double-decker in the Barton fleet! From there it was sold to Lloyd of Nuneaton, which was still operating it in 1978.

The Bedford VAL appeared at about the same time as the small-wheeled bicycle was in vogue. It, too, had wheels with a less-than-average diameter, in this case 16in. Although at this time there were two-axle 30ft long chassis available, many operators were attracted by the argument that if a blow-out occurred on one of the front tyres at high speed on the new motorways, then there was a safety factor about the VAL that its rivals did not possess. In that pre-Barbara Castle era when there were no speed restrictions on these new highways, the author recalls being whisked along the M45/1 in a Midland Red CM5T coach at 84mph on one occasion in torrential rain! The three axles of the lightweight VAL chassis allowed the load to be spread more lightly — another point of safety at high speeds. The VAL14 was powered by a normal vertical Leyland 400 unit placed in an orthodox position behind a front radiator. The Turner Manufacturing Company built under licence the American Clark five-speed synchromesh gearbox (with overdrive for the highest ratio).

At the 1962 Show two complete VALs were on display. One of these had a luxurious Plaxton Embassy II

44-seat body 36ft long and 8ft 2½in wide, whilst the other vehicle was of the same dimensions, but had a 52-seat Duple Vega Major body. The latter, registered 883 HMJ, did appear briefly on bus routes, including those of Edinburgh Corporation and King Alfred Motor Services of Winchester during 1963. That was the year when a third demonstrator, this time bearing a 53-seat *bus* body constructed by Willowbrook, appeared on the scene.

When the ninth British Coach Rally was held in April 1963 no less than 11 VALs took part. Amongst these were half a dozen bearing Plaxton's new Panorama or specially-designed Val bodywork. Other coachbuilders were now realising the potential market for these big vehicles, such as Yeates with its suitably adapted version of its Fiesta body and Harrington with its Legionnaire.

Most VALs had standard bodywork carrying 52 seats, but some operators packed more than this number into their vehicles. Barton took delivery in 1963 of seven Yeates-bodied dual-entrance buses. A. & C. Wigmore of Dinnington used 56-seat buses. North Western Road Car commissioned Strachans to supply oddly-shaped 52-seat buses on VAL14 chassis for their route 98, which passed under the very low Dunham Woodhouse bridge on the Bridgewater Canal. This had a clearance of a mere 8ft 9in. After they were withdrawn in 1971 some of them were shipped across to Ireland for further employment.

Weymann came up with a lavishly-designed body for the VAL, named the Topaz II, but this found few buyers, when it made its debut in 1965. Likewise Marshall-bodied VALs also remained rather a rarity, although it is worth noting that BEA bought three of these fitted with 40-seat central-entrance bus bodies for airport work.

Towards the end of 1967 a second version of the chassis, known as the VAL70, appeared at the SMT Show in Glasgow. It was powered by the new Bedford 466 diesel engine of 7.634 litres. In this instance the prototype bore a Duple Viceroy 36 body seating 52. This change of unit seems to have revitalised the VAL market, and 1968 saw quite a flood of orders for the new model. It was then that yet another coach builder entered the VAL field: the Portuguese firm of Caetano with its Estoril body, which sat 53 passengers in Continental luxury. However, few were sold, and none of these went to any of the major operators. Indeed the newly-established National Bus Company did not seem to favour the VAL, preferring the Bristol RE and the Leyland Leopard for its high-capacity coaches. Hence the NBC subsidiaries Southern Vectis and Hants & Dorset ceased to order VAL70s after the delivery of Nos 410/1 (SDL 743/4 J) and 1095/6 (WEL 804/5 J) respectively. Of the municipalities, only Edinburgh had taken anything

Above: One of North Western's famous VAL 14s with oddly-shaped Strachans body, designed to pass under the notorious Dunham Woodhouse bridge.

Facing page, upper: Early examples of Van Hool bodies imported to Britain from Belgium, on late-model VAL chassis.

Facing page, lower: Another later VAL, with attractive Duple Viceroy 37 bodywork, photographed against the dramatic shapes of Preston bus station.

Right: A rare combination — an early Moseley (Caetano) Estoril body on VAL chassis.

BEA used many of these Marshall-bodied VALs on airside duties at London's Heathrow Airport.

Volvo B58.

The last of the VAL70s to go into service just made it into the 'L' marks, such as HWD 531L of Webb (Armcote) and GAF 107L of Brown & Davies (Truro). Bedford had in 1972 introduced its two-axle YRT model to replace the VAL70, with its vertically-positioned engine amidships under the floor, and this satisfied the requirements of Wallace Arnold and Whittle.

As late as 1978 the VAL was still active in many of the smaller fleets of the independents. That summer it could be observed on hire to National Travel, which had rid its own fleets of these useful vehicles. Some more had been exported to Ireland, where they seemed to have become especially popular with scout troops! One was noted converted into a plush caravan by the manager of a small airfield in Lincolnshire.

The proprietor of Wilfreda Coaches of Ranskill (Notts) had the forethought and initiative to obtain the registration 1 VAL for his Duple Vega Major bodied VAL14, whilst Leon Motor Services of Doncaster had to be content with 448 VAL for its similarly-bodied No 64. Long may the memories of this unusual chassis be preserved. Doubtless by the time you read this article the first of the VAL14s will be appearing at some of the many vintage transport rallies, and I hope carrying off the trophies too!

like a real interest in the vehicle, and that interest waned after it had taken into its fleet Nos 228-30 (PSC 228-30G). Likewise the enthusiasm of the larger independents was also dwindling away by now. Apart from purchasing some secondhand machines, when it acquired the South Shields firm of Hall Bros, Barton had not bought any since its No 1000 had appeared in the demonstration park at Earls Court in 1964. Wallace Arnold, a staunch

supporter of the VAL from its earliest days, bought no more after its SUB 666-8G batch, whilst Yelloway of Rochdale had stopped taking delivery of this model a year earlier after it had received KDK 547 F. Whittle continued almost to the end with its last quartet being XAW 505/6/14/50 K. Instead these stalwarts had turned to a variety of alternatives. Yellowway had decided upon the AEC Reliance, whilst Harris of Grays was attracted to the

And then there were 49

Their numbers depleted by PTEs, mergers and take-overs, there are now only 49 local authority bus fleets in Britain. STEWART J. BROWN describes them.

There are 49 local authority bus fleets in Britain, owning between them just under 6,000 buses. District councils are responsible for the 37 English and nine Welsh undertakings; the three in Scotland are controlled by regional councils.

Sadly, the days of individuality in bus design have gone never to return, but there is probably more variety in local authority bus fleets than in any other group. Standardisation is the order of the day in the National Bus Company and to a lesser extent in the Scottish Bus Group. The PTEs inherited varied fleets but with each passing year standardisation ousts some of the variety. Even the independents are buying increasingly standardised vehicles from a small number of suppliers. Not, I hasten to add, that standardisation is wrong (if the standards are high enough) — but it can be boring!

The biggest local authority fleet is Lothian Region Transport — previously Edinburgh City Transport — which runs 615 vehicles. (All figures come from the 1978 *Little Red Book*.) Its double-deck fleet is made up entirely of Alexander-bodied Atlanteans (although

Titans are on order) but its comparatively small single-deck fleet features Leyland Leopards, Seddon Pennine midibuses, Ford Transit minibuses and a host of Duple-bodied Bedford coaches: VAS, VAM, YRQ, YRT and YMT.

Nottingham has the biggest English fleet with 400 buses, and has bought both Atlanteans and Fleetlines with distinctively styled bodywork by East Lancs, Northern Counties and Willowbrook. Nottingham's main claim to fame in recent times was an ambitious programme of fleet expansion allied to curbs on private cars in the city which, sad to relate, was not a success.

Moving down the league table we come to Cleveland Transit (which sounds as if it should be in Ohio) with 278 buses. Cleveland Transit is in fact the Langbaurgh, Middlesbrough and Stockton Joint Transport Committee. There are, incidentally, only two other joint undertakings, at Burnley and Pendle, and at Grimsby and Cleethorpes. Cleveland Transit was until 1974 Teeside Muncipal Transport; TMT was created on 1 April 1968 by the amalgamation of Middlesbrough Corporation, Stockton Corporation and Teeside Railless Traction Board. In 1974 Cleveland took over the independent Saltburn Motor Services, acquiring some quite un-municipal vehicles

Left: Nottingham bought a large fleet of lowheight AEC Renown chassis to which were fitted highbridge bodywork, in this case by Weymann.

Northern Counties bodywork of unusual appearance was specified by Cleveland Transit for its 1977 delivery of Bristol VRTs.

in the process. Fleetlines form the mainstay of the fleet but recent double-deckers include Bristol VRTs with lowheight Northern Counties bodies.

Kingston-upon-Hull comes next with 246 vehicles. From 1961 to 1975 all new double-deckers were Roe-bodied Atlanteans — though any resemblance between the first and final versions was purely coincidental! Hull then turned to the Metro-Scania Metropolitan and has the biggest municipal fleet of this model, running 50. Only three other local authorities (Leicester, Newport and Reading) run Metropolitans; there are 136 in municipal service.

Next it is convenient to take the other two Scottish regional undertakings. Grampian (244) and Tayside (229), previously Aberdeen and Dundee, have a common link in their choice of Alexander bodywork but their views on chassis diverge. Grampian takes an orthodox line, choosing Atlanteans. Tayside keeps its options open and currently favours Bristol VRTs and Ailsas: the latter model features in only one other local authority fleet, namely Derby. Grampian runs Scotland's only local authority Leyland Nationals.

Leicester runs 237 buses, and fairly conservative buses these were too until the 1970s when 35 Metro-Scania single-deckers were purchased, followed by 43 Metropolitan double-deckers. Leicester is the only English local authority to run single-deck Metro-Scanias — but they are used by three in Wales; to wit, Merthyr Tydfil, Newport and Taff Ely. Back to Leicester, and in October 1977 it became the first Dennis Dominator operator.

By virtue of its tramcar fleet, Blackpool is next on the list with 232 vehicles, 95 trams included. Conservatism was the keyword here with open-platform MCW Orion-bodied Titans entering service as late as 1968. In 1969 a complete about turn in policy introduced AEC Swifts with two-door Marshall bodies to the all-Titan fleet. Rear-engined double-deckers, in the shape of East Lancs-bodied Atlanteans, first appeared in 1977.

Cardiff (or Caerdydd to my Welsh readers) runs 229 buses. After experience with Fleetlines Cardiff has turned to Bristol VRTs in recent times, some of which have angular Willowbrook bodies.

Only one other fleet has over 200 buses. It is the furthest west and furthest south municipal bus fleet: Plymouth (217) where standardisation is the name of the game. If you see a double-decker here it's an Atlantean; the 60 single-deckers are all Leyland Nationals, the biggest fleet of Leyland's city bus in British municipal service.

Below the 200 figure come three neighbouring south

The first of 54 Guy Arab Vs delivered to Cardiff in the mid-1960s. This 1964 bus had Neepsend bodywork, and is seen in 1974 in the current orange livery with Welsh language offside fleetname.

Portsmouth bought several batches of rear-engined single-deckers in the 1960s and 1970s; there were Leyland Panther Cubs, Atlanteans and Nationals, and AEC Swifts with Marshall bodies like 180 shown here.

coast fleets: Southampton (196), Portsmouth (179) and Bournemouth (152). The first has standardised on East Lancs-bodied Atlanteans since 1968. Portsmouth favours the same chassis but goes all the way to Alexander of Falkirk for bodywork, as does Bournemouth which runs both Atlanteans and Fleetlines. Portsmouth is one of only three British operators to have bought Atlanteans with single-deck bodywork (the others were Birkenhead and Great Yarmouth). It received 12 such beasts, bodied by Seddon, in 1971. Two of the strangest vehicles in local authority service are Bournemouth's Strachans-bodied Bedford VAS3s, which have petrol engines.

Derby City Transport is actually just ahead of Bournemouth with 157 buses. Derby is an old-established Daimler customer and is currently running Fleetlines. The acquisition of Blue Bus Services in 1973 followed by the loss of the Blue Bus fleet in a depot fire in January 1976 brought a requirement for lowheight buses. This was met by Alexander-bodied Fleetlines of a style usually associated with the Scottish Bus Group, and a unique lowheight Ailsa. In March 1978 Derby became the first municipal buyer of a Foden-NC.

Two neighbouring fleets in highly municipalised Lancashire come next. There are 132 buses in the Burnley and Pendle Joint Transport fleet. Prior to 1974 this was the Burnley, Colne and Nelson undertaking which had been created in 1933 when the three towns' fleets were amalgamated. The fleet is mainly single-deck; Bristol VRTs purchased in 1976 were the first double-deckers for almost 10 years.

Nearby Blackburn (131) was enlarged in 1974 by being merged with neighbouring Darwen. This fleet supports local producers. Leyland supplies Atlantean chassis and East Lancs builds the bodies. East Lancs is, of course, a Blackburn company.

Reading's fleet (131) has a certain individuality. During the 1960s Reading pursued a policy of buying standee single-deckers. Early examples had two-door Burlingham bodies with deep side windows (so the standees could see out) and later purchases, regardless of bodybuilder, were designed to resemble the original Burlingham products. Reading then turned to 33ft long Bristol VRTs (nicknamed Jumbos because of their size) and later joined the small band of Metropolitan operators.

Daimlers feature in the 125-vehicle Chesterfield fleet

A 1967 Alexander-bodied Leyland Atlantean in the Grampian fleet entering Castle Street, Aberdeen in 1977.

which has a long-standing low bridge problem and until 1977 included some side-gangway lowbridge buses. The last of these were 1961 Leyland Titans. Current deliveries are Fleetlines, although odd secondhand Panthers have also joined the fleet.

Newport (104) is one of three Welsh operators of Metro-Scanias and, with 44, has the largest fleet of this model in Britain. It also has 10 Metropolitan double-deckers. Before buying Anglo-Swedish buses Newport had favoured an Anglo-Scottish product: Leyland Atlanteans with Alexander bodies. Newport is another of the few municipalities to have taken over an independent in recent times, in this case a stage service operated by A B Smith of Newport, along with a pair of Bedfords, in 1974.

And so to the under-100 fleets. Preston has 98 buses and since Leyland's factory is just outside the town it comes as no surprise to find a 97% Leyland fleet — and the exceptions, a trio of Bristol LHSs, are still Leyland group products. The mainstay of the fleet are 41 Panthers, five of which have rare Marshall Camair bodies and were built for the defunct Stratford Blue company. Before the Panthers Preston bought Titans; since the Panther's demise 33ft long

Atlanteans have been added to the fleet.

The next two fleets are on the east coast and are both amalgamations of smaller undertakings. Grimsby and Cleethorpes Transport Joint Committee (98) was formed in January 1957; each town had previously operated its own buses. Grimsby-Cleethorpes bought the last AEC Swifts to be built. Hartlepool (89) dates from April 1967 when the West Hartlepool fleet was amalgamated with that of four-bus Hartlepool. All post-1965 additions to what is now the Hartlepool fleet have been single-deckers. Hartlepool was one of the first purchasers of the Bristol RE/ECW combination when it was made available on the open market in 1967; it now buys Leyland Nationals.

Southend Transport (80) buys Fleetlines. Not so long ago it had Lowlanders (the only other municipal Lowlanders ran for Luton) and secondhand Worldmasters. It was also the last English municipal operator of lowbridge buses; the final survivor, a 1958 Leyland PD3 with Massey body, was withdrawn in March 1978. When the last of the exposed-radiator Titans (F-registered) has gone the only thing worth visiting Southend for will be, with respect, the fine pier railway . . .

But I digress. On to Northampton which does not even have a pier. For some 30 years Northampton (84) bought little else but Roe-bodied Daimlers. I can visualise a standing order with both companies: 'Same as last year please'. The last were delivered in 1968 and were quite historic buses: the last CVG6s built for Britain; the last teak-framed Roe bodies; the last buses with preselector gearboxes; and the last buses with open rear platforms. Perhaps the shock of finding in 1969 that the 'Same as last year' was no longer available explains why no more new buses were bought until 1973 . . . The latest additions to the fleet are Alexander-bodied VRTs, the only examples of this combination in England.

Strange as it may seem, Ipswich (77) bought its first motorbus in 1950. From 1923 to 1950 all its buses were trolleys. For 16 years AECs only were bought; now the ubiquitous Atlantean is replacing the familiar Regents. Warrington (76) was a Bristol RE purchaser but has recently favoured Fleetlines and Atlanteans. Warrington is probably best known for its sizeable fleet of Fodens, the last of which survived until 1972.

Lancaster City Transport (74) was formed in 1974 and incorporates the previously separate Lancaster and Morecambe & Heysham undertakings. A fleet of Alexander-bodied Leyland Leopards has been built up since the amalgamation and Atlanteans currently on order will be the first new double-deckers since 1965.

Now for the railway towns. Swindon, famous as the Great Western Railway's town, is served by Thamesdown Transport which currently runs a Fleetline fleet. Darlington, which was linked to Stockton by the world's first railway (depending on your definition of 'first') has a 69-strong bus fleet and, like Ipswich, ran only trolleybuses until 1950. After buying conventional Guy and Daimler chassis Darlington tried the unsuccessful Roadliner, the single-deck Fleetline and the short-lived Seddon RU before becoming, in 1977, the first operator to order single-deck Dennis Dominators.

From north-east England to south Wales and Rhymney Valley (68), a creation of 1974's local government reorganisation which combined the fleets of Bedwas & Machen, Caerphilly and Gelligaer. A mixed fleet was acquired; the present standard is the Leyland Leopard. Nearby Merthyr Tydfil (66) is the largest all-single-deck local authority fleet. Its last double-deckers were sold in 1977. Until 1972 Leyland Leopards were purchased, followed by two Metro Scanias, four Bristol REs, and then small batches of Leyland Nationals.

Barrow-in-Furness (64) is the only local authority operator in Cumbria. Here Leyland Nationals, manufactured at nearby Workington, are currently being added to the fleet and no double-deckers have

been purchased since 1961. For a brief period from 1972 Barrow was involved in coach operation when it purchased the business of Hadwin of Ulverston. The Hadwin fleet retained its separate identity and was sold in 1977.

Also with 64 buses, Brighton is the only fleet which is entirely double-deck. It is also 100% Leyland, including some unusual omo conversions of front-engined Titans. Paradoxically, Brighton was in September 1977 the first operator outside London to try Leyland's second-generation rear-engined Titan TN15 in passenger service.

The most easterly local authority fleet is Great Yarmouth (60). In 1964 this undertaking purchased the last Daimler Freelines built; these survived until 1977 and were probably the last of their type to run in Britain. It also ran a trio of Atlanteans with unusual Marshall single-deck bodywork. In the 1970s AEC Swifts were added to the fleet followed by ECW-bodied Bristol VRTs which looked particularly attractive in Great Yarmouth livery.

Another seaside resort comes next. Eastbourne (59) currently favours Leyland's Atlantean but its main claim to fame is that it was Britain's first municipal bus operator — in 1903 which was a little bit before my time . . .

Maidstone followed a fairly conventional vehicle policy for a 58-bus undertaking until 1975 when it forsook Atlanteans for Bedfords and surplus Nottingham Leopards which retained their distinctive lilac livery.

After experience of Panthers and REs Lincoln City Transport turned to ECW-bodied VRTs. Few municipal fleets have purchased Portuguese Caetano bodywork but in 1975 this was Lincoln's choice for a now withdrawn Bedford YRT coach.

Colchester (53), the oldest town in England, runs one of the most modern fleets with no buses over 12 years old. Its current standard is the comparatively unusual combination of Atlantean chassis and ECW body.

Hyndburn (53) was a new name which appeared in 1974 to oust the familiar Accrington. Although the name was changed Accrington's striking navy and red livery survived as one of the few individual liveries in these days of uniformity. Every bus in the fleet has East Lancs bodywork and recent deliveries have been Atlanteans. Hyndburn received one of the three unusually-styled coach bodies produced by East Lancs in 1974/75: the other two went to Halton.

The last two of the '50 and over' fleets are also in the north west. Rossendale Transport (52) was until 1974 a joint transport committee formed when the Haslingden and Rawtenstall fleets were merged in 1968. Here too the entire fleet has East Lancs

Preston rebuilt a number of Leyland-bodied PD2s as 30ft-long forward entrance buses in the early 1960s. This one is seen entering the town's bus station in 1977.

bodywork. Chester has 50 buses and at present favours Fleetlines and Leopards. It was the last British operator to buy a new Guy bus. The last, an Arab V with Northern Counties body, entered service in 1969.

And so to the small fleets. Halton is another of those names with an unfamiliar ring — it was until 1974 Widnes. It is the smallest English operator to have purchased Leyland Nationals. East Staffordshire sounds a rather grand name for a fleet of 41 buses serving Burton-on-Trent. This is another Fleetline fleet and has the dubious honour of having for many years standardised on Gardner's miserly 5LW engine. Indeed, the last five-cylinder engined buses built were Daimler CCG5s delivered to Burton in 1968. By 1978 a more adventurous vehicle policy was in evidence with the purchase of both Atlanteans and Dominators.

The smallest English district council fleet? Fylde. This was until 1974 Lytham St Annes and recent additions to the 39 vehicle fleet have been new and second-hand Leyland Atlanteans. Fylde is also an active coach operator and uses Leyland Leopards for this work.

However, that is not the end of the story. Wales provides five more local authority fleets. In south Wales, Cynon Valley and Taff Ely each have 38 vehicles. The former used to be Aberdare and its fleet is now entirely single-deck; the latter was Pontypridd. Both own Leyland Nationals and Taff Ely can also boast a trio of Metro-Scanias. Pontypridd was the last buyer of AEC Regents before that model's demise in 1968 and it has not bought any double-deckers since.

Islwyn Borough Council (30), like the two in the previous paragraph, dates from 1974 and was previously the West Monmouthshire Omnibus Board, controlled by Bedwellty and Mynyddislwyn urban district councils. Here the standard bus is the Willowbrook-bodied Leopard and there is only a handful of deckers, all Titans with side-gangway lowbridge bodies.

Last and least come the two north Wales district council fleets. Aberconwy, or Llandudno as it used to be, runs 10 buses including a pair of unique Dennis Pax purchased in 1968. The minute Colwyn fleet comprises one Bedford VAS and an A series Ford which provide a summer season service.

So much for the present, but what of the future? Both large and small municipalities have shown a willingness to try sophisticated buses. The Leyland National features in 13 fleets; the Metro-Scania/Metropolitan in six. But the majority favour orthodoxy — Fleetlines, Atlanteans and VRTs for double-deckers and Leopards for single-deckers. None of these models has a long life ahead. The Leopard is an operator's bus in that it is of proven reliability but, with its high floor level, it can hardly be called an ideal urban passenger's bus. Perhaps the simpler Series B Leyland National will be an answer.

Leyland's new Titan, originally intended to replace the three existing double-deck models, is somewhat different in concept from the previous Titan and is unlikely to appeal to most local authority operators until a simplified version becomes available. There can be little doubt that some municipalities will opt for the Dennis Dominator and, perhaps, MCW's Metrobus. In municipal ownership there is only one Foden-NC and, outside its native Scotland, one Ailsa; both run for Derby. Other municipal buyers for both models seem unlikely at the time of writing.

Indeed, in the smaller fleets the future of the double-decker looks uncertain in the face of a continuing decline in the number of passengers carried and it is possible in moments of pessimism to visualise an increasing number of all-single-deck fleets. And on that sad note, I'll leave you.

Before Selnec

R. L. WILSON photographs illustrate the buses of the eleven municipal fleets which on 1 November 1969 passed into the hands of the new Selnec (South-east Lancashire, north-east Cheshire) PTE.

With 1,250 buses, Manchester Corporation was the biggest of Selnec's constituents. When this Daimler COG5 with MCT/Crossley 54-seat body was photographed at Hyde Road depot in 1961 it was the last prewar Manchester bus still operational.

Below: Salford contributed 271 buses to Selnec, but not this 1951 Daimler CVG6, one of a large fleet with 54-seat MCW bodies; it was withdrawn a few months before Selnec's vesting day. It is seen in 1961 in a special Civic Week reversed livery.

A reminder of the interesting Bolton fleet (249 buses in 1969). It was a Leyland Tiger TS8c with Park Royal body, seen in Portland Street, Manchester in 1953.

Foot of page: Bury Corporation (96 buses) bought a small batch of these Leyland Titan PD2/37s with East Lancs bodies in 1967, for a service where a weight restriction prevented the use of rear-engined vehicles. One is seen in the centre of Bury in 1969.

The small, blue-painted Leigh fleet (57 buses) required low-height vehicles, like this 1959 Dennis Loline II with 72-seat East Lancs body, at Leigh bus station in 1968.

Unlike its Leyland-dominated brothers, Rochdale (130 buses) was a keen AEC user. This 1951 AEC Regal IV with East Lancs 44-seat body is seen in Liverpool in 1956, painted in the 'streamlined' blue and cream livery of the time.

Ashton-under-Lyne (60 buses) inter-worked trolleybuses with Manchester until 1966. This 1950 Crossley Empire TDD42/1 with Crossley 58-seat body is seen turning into Portland Street, Manchester in 1954, when it was painted in this ornate blue, red and cream livery.

Locally-produced Crossleys were familiar around the Manchester area for many years. This all-Crossley DD42/3 of Oldham Corporation (180 buses) is seen in Manchester in 1950.

The Stalybridge, Hyde, Mossley and Dukinfield Transport and Electricity Board was, thankfully, more often simply known as SHMD (91 buses), and pursued an individual vehicle buying policy. This Daimler Freeline G6H, new in 1953, had a Northern Counties 34-seat standee body, and is seen at Stalybridge in 1966.

Smallest Selnec constituent was Ramsbottom UDC, with 12 buses, always Leylands from 1928 right through to Selnec days; in fact Ramsbottom ordered the very last front-engined Leyland Titan, delivered to Selnec in 1969. This 1950 all-Leyland PD2/3 56-seater is seen in 1967 at Holcombe Brook.

Right: How the rot began for John Aldridge: the London bus centenary parade.

Stockport (148 buses) received a number of these Massey-bodied utility Guy Arabs in 1944. Bus 212 is seen in the Mersey Square depot in 1958.

I Was There

After 21 years as a transport journalist, JOHN ALDRIDGE recalls some of the interesting transport events he has witnessed, and some of the vehicles he has seen.

My downfall was probably the clash of dates between the last morning for revision before the Law Society's examinations and the London General centenary parade in 1956 in Regents Park.

The centenary parade won.

In fact I had already been selling the odd news picture to the transport press, and by January 1958 I had changed intended career and — partly through the kindly offices of the late William Lambden — become a full-time staff member of the old *Bus & Coach* and its larger companion, *Motor Transport*.

But life as a junior, junior underthing is not all idyllic, of course, and there are many routine chores. The chores still remain, but over the years as you learn and can be trusted, then more interesting tasks can come your way.

Not that I have ever done badly, having ridden, for example, on the last Hastings trolleybus, and the last Swansea and Mumbles tram. More recently I have stood under the first Leyland B15 prototype, with its bodywork still a shell, as Leyland Truck and Bus chief Ron Ellis explained the ideas and the hopes it represented.

Some of the B15 ideas were not entirely new to me, because one Joe McGowan of Leyland had a hand in B15's design, and for several years I had sat opposite him at lunch, during five years or so I spent at Leyland, as editor of *Leyland Journal*. We used to talk about some of the failings of the bus business and bus designs.

Which brings me to another advantage of being a transport journalist: you mix with them all — drivers, conductors, inspectors, traffic managers, engineers, general managers, sales managers ... And that should give you a splendid insight into the whole industry. Another attraction, too, is the feeling of being informed, of knowing something about events before they happen or are even announced.

But it is not all just jolly, jolly fun and interest. After every event is over, and you have travelled back home — perhaps hundreds of miles — you have to sit down and write about it, and probably more briefly than you would wish. Particularly if you work on a weekly paper, there is no time to sit and think.

Probably the greatest attraction of the job is the comparative freedom it involves: it's not nine to five work by any means, but you have the freedom to make your own arrangements for combining jobs or visits, perhaps to go there that way, so that you can have a ride on the new High Speed Train. That, incidentally, was one which didn't work for me, because the previous day a freight train had ripped up more than two miles of track, and the ride to Swindon was on a very slow High Speed Train, and the ride back, a motor coach to Reading, and then an ordinary train.

A final advantage of the job, if you are interested in transport generally, and most transport journalists are, is that *somebody else is paying the fare*.

What goes on behind the scenes is fascinating, though one must always beware of knowing lots, and telling readers little. They pay their money to be informed. But there are always snippets of information, which it may not be prudent to use at the time, yet which, with a good memory, you should store away in your mind, for use later.

In Septemebr 1978, for example, Gardner announced its new engine, the 6LXC, an uprated version of the 6LX. The announcement was done in typically Gardner fashion, with very little detail indeed, and what's more, few if any hints had been dropped before then, even to the vehicle makers themselves.

This secrecy is, I think, a mistake and it took my mind back many years to the announcement of the Gardner 6LX engine. That also was a too closley guarded secret that indirectly lost Guy Motors and Gardner a lot of business. By the time the 6LX was announced, the East Kent Road Car had ordered AEC Regent Vs and in fact went on to standardise on them for several years.

East Kent had wanted to keep with Guy double-deckers, being happy with the large fleet it had. Unfortunately, Guy could only offer the 6LW, which East Kent's chief engineer rightly thought insufficiently powerful for a 30ft long double-decker. And neither he, nor Guy, knew anything about the forthcoming bigger engine, so the order went to AEC, and the next, and the next . . .

New designs, and new models are always interesting, and the run-up to commercial show time, whether at Earls Court, Kelvin Hall, or the National Exhibition Centre, Birmingham, can be exciting. It's certainly busy.

A vintage year for such announcements was 1973, when in succeeding weeks at the end of September and beginning of October three of us from different journals found ourselves successively hearing about Ailsa's new front-engined double-decker and MCW's new rear-engined double-decker.

The Ailsa story was particularly memorable because it was done with typical Ailsa style and *panache*. We flew from London to Glasgow, were met there and taken to a Scottish loch where we boarded Jim McKelvie's yacht — a large Volvo-engined ocean-going yacht that he had designed and built himself — for a short cruise and evening meal.

During all this we had the undivided attention of the few people who had designed the bus. Chats like this, with virtually no interruptions, help give a much better insight into how and why something is done the way it is. I recall the chats they in turn had had with engineering staff in bus garages here, there and everywhere, at which emerged not only the traditional engineer's dislike of rear engines but also some of the other unnecessarily difficult jobs in bus maintenance such as removing the rear axle of a vehicle. As a result that task is easy on an Ailsa.

It was not until next morning that we saw the hardware — the first complete (or nearly) underframe, and that of course was back on dry land, at the factory.

It was dark, raining or drizzling, for most of the cruise, by the way.

A week later, the Metropolitan was quite a contrast, as we more or less started the day at Washwood Heath with a ride on the first completed vehicle, which was MCW's first entry into other than the bodywork field for buses.

Over the six years since then, MCW has probably done rather better, with its rear-engine designs. Perhaps Ailsa — now Volvo — made the mistake of not merely talking to people and learning from them, but of believing them. Despite all the problems — mainly, I suppose, transmission ones — with rear engines, the people who count, general managers, chief engineers, director-generals of passenger transport executives, and others have preferred the devil they knew. And that I suppose is what makes making things and selling them such a chancy business.

I learnt much about this when I was at Leyland in the early and mid-1960s, and it is an experience that was an eye-opener. Many an enthusiast — and some journalists, too — forget that vehicle makers have to make some profits. Unfair press comments or unnecessary criticism can lose sales. Equally, if there are genuine criticisms and complaints about a product or a service, it is part of a trade paper's duty to do something about it. The paper should reflect the needs of its readers.

Early Leyland Nationals, you may recall, suffered more than their fair share of failures, mainly of the small, irritating and needless kind. Most, in fact, were the result of shortcomings of suppliers to the Leyland

Swansea & Mumbles tram, alas no more.

National plant rather than the maker itself. But there were no signs at all of the manufacturer making much effort to remedy them, and by-and-by all sorts of influential people in the bus business including a PTE's chief engineer were asking if *Motor Transport's Bus & Coach* section could not help.

The outcome was an open letter to the Leyland National management, which appeared prominently in the *Bus & Coach* section. Reply — and wrath — from the bus builder was swift, but somewhat muted when we produced (with identities removed) a considerable number of letters from our readers all agreeing with what had been said and adding further snags that they had encountered. Of course, we published the maker's reply, plus one or two letters from readers, and great efforts were made to improve the vehicle's reliability.

But the open letter caught the eye of a big New Zealand undertaking which had been about to buy some, and it opted for Mercedes Benz 0.305s instead, a point that Ron Ellis never ceased to remind me of, whenever we subsequently met.

My experiences when I was at Leyland a decade earlier broadened my outlook considerably. It made me look at buses in an international light, perhaps like the British tram fans who turned their attentions overseas, when British trams all but vanished. But there the parallel ends.

The economics of production dictate that a manufacturer must have a wide market, if not for his actual individual models, then for their components. Leyland, Mercedes, Volvo and many others are experts at this art, though as the years go by it becomes more and more difficult as nationalism appears to become stronger and every country wants to build its own vehicles.

One of the most interesting overseas visits I made, wearing a Leyland hat, was to Copenhagen Tramways, which had run some 'Leylands' for several years and had just placed a big order to buy hundreds of DAB-built single-deckers to replace its trams. The oldest trams, incidentally, were scrapped, and the newest ended up in Alexandria, Egypt.

DAB is a Danish chassis and bodybuilder, owned by Leyland, and the buses it built at that time were basically Leyland Worldmaster running units, with some Continental components as well, incorporated into a DAB-designed structure.

One fascinating feature of Copenhagen Tramways was its flat-fare token system. If you bought tokens in bulk, from slot machines or other sources, you got a

much cheaper ride, though even in those days the flat fare was about three times what you would have paid in Britain for an average two-or three-fare stage journey.

The token idea, with the self-service Bell Punch-made machines into which passengers placed them, caught the eye of the late Norman Morton, then general manager at Sunderland Corporation. After visits by him, by Sunderland councillors and by transport department staff, Sunderland adopted the system, though unfortunately it was a failure there.

Yet flat fares are still widespread in transport systems the world over.

Reverting to the DAB buses, one feature of the factory at Silkeborg at the time was the very restricted space. They used to build chassis frames upstairs, and then lower them to the ground floor. Though the Copenhagen design was partly a special, you can find similar vehicles elsewhere, for example in Geneva, Switzerland, where the local undertaking bought them because they were much cheaper than the local Swiss-built product. Today, the twist to that situation is that DAB fits Swiss-built Saurer engines into some of its models, including the articulated design, one of which was seen here in 1977 after previously going to a transport congress in Canada.

Another overseas visit in my Leyland days was to a Schwyz, Switzerland, operator who was very satisfied

with a batch of Orlandi-bodied Worldmasters, which incidentally carried ski-racks at the rear in winter. The operator's transport interests were widespread, including a ski lift and a funicular railway, and, in order to obtain some good pictures, I was given a driver and bus for the afternoon.

But I think the highlight of that trip was the ride up from the railway station to the town, on the operator's old-fashioned bonneted Saurer, more like a limousine than a public service vehicle.

Another overseas trip, to Sweden, to Stockholm, was made just after Leyland obtained its big order for rear-engined single-deckers and also Atlanteans, when the country required a large number of new vehicles all at once, because of the changeover — in 1967 — to driving on the right.

Then Stockholm ran lots of Scania Vabis buses — great long vehicles they were — fitted with torque convertors. and they gave me a prejudice that I still have against such transmissions. There seemed to be many revs, and much work, in return for little apparent speed, at least when moving off.

However, enough of foreign stories, which form only a minute part of one's work. More frequent events, for example, are visits to new bus stations or garages, or the coach rallies, or the bus-driver-of-the-year finals, or transport conferences.

Calls on independent operators can be fascinating,

too, and one never knows quite what to expect. Some are run with a precision that should be the envy of company operators, while others apparently succeed in making a living where it would appear impossible.

Independent operators are, as a group, those about whom least is heard. Visiting them is sometimes not without its pitfalls and problems, for example when you discover that 'he's had to go out driving'.

Their methods of operation can be interesting though with some things happen rather than get planned. But almost without exception those in rural areas with stage services have, at least until the last few years, put in their own money and resources with no hope of any financial return.

The big concern which talks of non-paying services has at least paid its staff and managers the rate for the job, but many an independent has worked long hours unpaid mainly out of a sense of loyalty to the local community.

Off the beaten track, and a little away from the eyes of the enforcement staff of the traffic commissioners, one can come across strange practices, such as one conductor to three rear-platform double-deckers (two of which were running as duplicates), or the double-decker conducted — in admirable fashion — for part of the way by a small boy. At the other end of the long straggling village the conductress — his mother — got on. Her first act was not to collect fares, but to comb his hair.

Then there was the small bus operator in a holiday resort who looked after me in splendid fashion and treated me to an excellent lunch, leaving his car outside the restaurant, parked on yellow lines: 'they all know my car,' he said. And in one sense, that provides the clue to why small operators do so much for their communities. They have a certain standing and a sense of belonging.

One of the attractions of the job is the uncertainty: tomorrow just might bring a routine invitation to a London press conference . . . or a trip to the Orkneys. You never know.

One such invitation, by phone, was to go and look at and drive the Moulton eight-wheeler coach, a vehicle I knew little about, and had seen only in a picture. Well, it has a ride, and stability, quite unrivalled and unequalled by anything else I have ever ridden on, and one can only regret that now even Dennis have dropped the plans to build it.

The Moulton relies on square-tube section and a suspension syustem using gas- or liquid-filled cylinders as on BMC 1100 or Maxi cars, and was originally developed to provide at modest development cost, a BMC psv chassis using existing mechanical units as far as possible.

Above: A day out from the Loughview Hotel at Larne in 1925, with a fine Maudslay charabanc, and several Fords.

Holidaymakers at Rhyl in 1923 seem more interested in the Punch and Judy show than in the Brookes Bros (White Rose) Leyland G7 double-decker.

Weather
Permitting....

Above: Undaunted by snow, a Bedford VAL/Duple demonstrator on test in 1963.

No problems for a 1937 Brush car in a Blackpool sandstorm, but the sweeper seems to be fighting a losing battle.

Snow problems for Northern General in 1978 — an abandoned Routemaster (*above*) and a snowbound Leyland National (*below*).

Upper right: A foggy day in Congleton, with a Potteries ex-Rowbottom Foden PVD6/Massey. *Lower right:* Floods in Godalming in 1968, with a Blue Saloon Ford/Harrington and a Southdown Leopard/Plaxton on rail emergency services.

A snowstorm in Edinburgh in 1968 with
an Eastern Scottish 76-seat Bristol/ECW
Lodekka passing the distinguished
ironwork of St Andrew Square.

Sightseeing goes on all year in Paris,
even when it snows. A Paris Vision
Saviem with a French interpretation of a
double-deck body, in 1969.

Harrington's Cavalier Approach

The coach bodies built by Harrington were widely admired, and are sadly missed. RAY STENNING remembers their Indian Summer.

When it comes to superlatives one often hears talk of the Rolls-Royce of this, or Rolls-Royce of that. It usually means that what's being described transcends normal criteria and can only really be judged by its own standards.

Harrington could be regarded as the Rolls-Royce of coachbuilders — certainly in quality and workmanship. Its styles produced since the advent of the underfloor-engined chassis reflected a philosphy of superb craftsmanship, a fine line and a deftly-proportioned classic elegance that was at the same time completely modern.

The word *graceful* has a dowdy smudge to it. I prefer to describe the Harrington line as sensitive, fluent, expressive, occasionally beautiful. It had style and breeding (qualities subtly understated); in an equally uncomfortable word, it had *class*! Even the model names conjured up images of chivalry, brave deeds, heroism. And they sounded handsome — Cavalier, Grenadier, Crusader, Legionnaire; legendary stuff!

Although a few years ago the ranks of British coachbuilders seemed to be thinning down to just Plaxton and Duple, the re-emergence of Willowbrook and rise in popularity in Britain of Van Hool and the Alf Moseley imports, makes one wonder if Harrington's demise from the coach body market in 1965 might not have been inevitable after all.

Inevitable, unfortunate, untimely, the victim of circumstance, or whatever, Harrington is now regretfully part of history. The Hove, Sussex, based firm made its first major excursion into bodying the then new underfloor-engined chassis in the early 1950s with the Wayfarer. Some versions perpetuated that Harrington peculiarity, the dorsal fin. It was basically a styling gimmick, despite any claims as an important ventilation component, and part of the flamboyant feeling of the time in automobile and coach styling — an unfortunate, in retrospect though marvellous at the time, backlash from wartime austerity. This odd appendage was even included as

late as 1958 on a Wayfarer Mk IV coach, SAM 47, for the famous Silver Star of Porton Down, near Salisbury.

The Wayfarer had its loyal retinue — one almost feels entitled to use 'Maidstone & District' as an adjective for the model, especially for the Mk IV, since that operator was totally faithful to the style for much of the 1950s. Southdown, in whose territory Harrington was situated, surprisingly shunned the later developments, preferring the 'grande-dame' looks produced by Beadle and Duple.

It was the Wayfarer's successor that grabbed the attention of the coach world in 1960 and brought many more operators knocking at Harrington's door. When the Cavalier was unveiled it was quite sensational, and widely acclaimed. Duple was still fiddling around with adaptions of the Super Vega for the

underfloor-engined chassis — the Britannia and its Donnington derivative. Plaxton was beginning to formulate its later very popular Panorama but had yet to get the design ingredients just right. The Harrington Cavalier was the bridge between the traditional way to style a coach (the drooping 'ball-gown' look) and new concepts that were soon to be expressed in metal and glass. It was a happy marriage between the sensuality of curved lines and the powerful visual effect of sharp angles.

Originally produced to the then maximum permissible length of 30ft, the Cavalier was later offered in a 36ft version. The first production Cavalier at this length went to Grey-Green, 409 DLD, and this coach is thought to have inaugurated the first operation of a 36-footer on daily express service in Britain, in 1962. The Cavalier also became available in a 31ft 5in version.

To design successfully a body with a dipping waistline, still able to fit different length chassis without totally different panels, and not to look 'added to' or 'a bit lopped off' is not easy. Harrington's solution was to increase the length of the first (deeper) side window bay (the one immediately behind the door) for the 31ft 5in version; and for the 36ft version this and an additional (straight) window bay inserted immediately after the second bay (after the first on the raised waist line). The clever trick lay in the fact that the waistrail dip didn't start until the third window bay (see diagram). It was all very subtly executed, and the sort of thing only an analytical type of mind like mine would notice!

The Cavalier was aptly named, for it had that courtly courteous air to it. Its manners seemed beyond reproach and yet it also managed to convey the other things associated with the name — it was dashing, handsome, immaculate and spirited. Cavaliers could be seen dashing about their business in many corners of the land, especially as touring coaches — with Greenslades in the West Country, Southdown in Sussex, Ribble up in Lancashire, with Northern General in the north-east, to mention a few. Although the Cavalier had little in common with the Wayfarer, it looked a Harrington.

The Grenadier came out for the 1962 Commercial Motor Show and was a logical development from the Cavalier, which continued to be available. Some customers even specified a strange mixture of the two. Southdown had 31ft 5in Grenadiers with Cavalier lower front panels (it had a sizeable fleet of Cavaliers of all lengths) which did look rather nice. Orange Luxury (George Ewer) had at least one Grenadier with a Cavalier windscreen to enable a roof destination box to be fitted; and Grey Cars (the Devon General coach fleet) bought some 31ft 5in Cavaliers with Grenadier lower front panels but to an overall width of 7ft 6in.

The Grenadier was a striking visual statement — it had the same fine look, but was sharper, more aggressive, and best suited to the

The heavy lines of the Wayfarer body; a Southdown Royal Tiger, on loan to Aldershot & District, in 1966.

An integral Harrington Contender, with 8-cylinder Rolls-Royce petrol engine and automatic gearbox.

longer chassis where the Cavalier had tended to look a little stretched. I must admit the Grenadier at the shorter length could sometimes appear a bit dumpy, but to an untrained or less critical eye this just wouldn't be noticed.

Main differences from the Cavalier were longer fixed windows (pressure ventilation was used) and a 'meaner'-looking front. Frontal mouldings, air intakes, grille, destination aperture, etc were redesigned and the windscreen was taller with a sharp peak over the top. Harrington intended to fit a similar screen to the Cavalier originally, but Triplex at that time was unable to mass-produce such a large screen satisfactorily — Harrington ideas being in advance of the technology needed to bring them to fruition! (as so often in the past). Once again it was mainly the BET companies that bought the Grenadier in quantity —

Southdown, M&D, Trent, Northern, Black & White, for example.

Harrington also bodied the front-engined lightweights with what I consider to be an infinitely more attractive design than the contemporary Duple or Plaxton styles (and certainly Yeates). This was the Crusader (oh those gallant names!) and had all the Harrington hallmarks of balance, stylishness and that air of quality — class, as I apologetically described it earlier. The early Crusaders combined elements of the Wayfarer, especially the windscreen, front quarters and the basic look of the front, with a foretaste of the Cavalier — the forward-sloping pillar, the rear end and the general feel of the side.

Although aimed at the independent market, it also penetrated Southdown's fleet on no less than 30 Commer Avenger chassis — Southdown also had

An early Crusader body, on Commer Avenger chassis for the Southdown fleet.

Below: The final Crusader variant, a 1964 Bedford SB in the Grey-Green fleet.

The severity was carried a little too far on the first version, since the roof contour was squared in section, producing an uncomfortable flat panel at cant level. However, for the 1964 Show (Harrington's last appearance) the roof contour was changed into a beautiful shallow arch. Fixed side windows also became standard, and it now looked quite stunning, but way ahead of its time. Put alongside contemporary Plaxton and Duple products, the Legionnaire was clean, completely sharp, and full of subtle design details that perpetuated the Harrington look.

By the early 1970s the public was beginning to appreciate the visual potency of the straight line and sharp angle, more so as the decade progressed, but in 1963/4 the light was too bright. It is a great pity, for the Legionnaire was beautiful to travel in, and with development over the years could have been seen in the same numbers as Duple and Plaxton were, instead of the disappointingly few that were actually built. One thinks of the Foreign Legion and its lost souls — could the name have been an omen?

Harrington had plans to extend the Legionnaire idea to the underfloor-engined chassis, but this came to nought since a decision was made to withdraw from the market altogether in 1965. This had nothing to do with any failures or lack of orders — Harrington had a healthy order book. It needed capital investment to expand, and expansion was its only course for survival, but the Rootes Group, which controlled Harrington, was not inclined to invest in that direction. So Harrington passed out of the coachbuilding scene, on top — which is the only way to go!

It was a great pity from an aesthetic point of view, and for the enthusiast, as had it survived we would be witnessing some interesting developments in coach body design today. Always innovators, always abreast of the times and very often far ahead (Harrington's wartime experience with airframe construction and the multitude of other things the backroom boys later dabbled in —

15 Avengers with Burlingham Seagull coachwork, amongst its more usual Leyland Tiger Cubs and Leopards.

The Mk III Crusader introduced at the 1962 London Commerical Motor Show (along with the Grenadier) was basically an adaption of the Grenadier to suit the lightweights. It was a little heavy around the front with a wrap-around screen and a rather unhappy grille and headlight panel. Otherwise it was a very attractive coach, but no match for the superb Duple Bella Vega, which was taking this market by storm.

The final Crusader, the 1964 Mk IV, was visually a bit of a mess. It had no coherent look to it, being an unsatisfactory combination of misapplied design elements — I can't say kinder than that. It tried to give the appearance of a modern version of the original Crusader, but really it was a ghastly caricature of

the once elegant style. Ten out of ten for trying! A strange customer for the Crusader Mk IV was the South Midland part of Thames Valley, which purchased three Bedford SB13s with this coachwork towards the end of 1964. This was the first instance of Harrington coachwork on a new vehicle for a Tilling company since United Automobile's six Bristol L6B coaches in 1950! The Crusader's market penetration was small.

Penetrating, or should it be just brushing, a new market, a completely fresh model appeared on the scene in 1963 — the marvellous Legionnaire, a severe style for the Bedford VAL and new Ford Thames 36 chassis. For dramatic effect the Legionnaire relied on a completely straight waistline, totally rectangular side windows, and the by then Harrington trademark of a sharp peak over the tall windscreen.

you wouldn't believe half of them —
gave it a lead in welded construction
techniques and the extensive use of
light alloys; also glass-fibre moulding
— remember the Sunbeam Alpine
specials?). Harrington will always be
remembered for the very things I
sentimentally expressed earlier — or
in its own slogan, *Comfort, Quality,
Craftsmanship.*

What took the place of Harrington
style in the coach world? Well Duple
had similar ideas with its
Commander Mk III and IV — but you
know about that one from last year's
Buses Annual. The Belgian Van Hool
firm has been going in the same
direction with considerable success,
but comparisons from one
generation to another, over a gap of
15 years (yes, really that long ago!),
are dangerous. Aesthetic standards
move forward, taste leaps forward
and backward with alarming
contrariety, but in its time, in
retrospect, Harrington could be
called the Rolls-Royce of
coachbuilders.

Above: The impressive Grenadier body,
an AEC Reliance chassis in the Maidstone
& District fleet.

Below: The sadly short-lived Legionnaire
body, on Ford Thames 36 chassis for Aer
Lingus, at Heathrow in 1965.

Development and Determination. An Ulsterbus AEC Reliance with Alexander-style UTA body passes under the Shipquay Gate on a Londonderry city service in 1968.

Looking Back at Tracky. The final pre-NBC Yorkshire Traction livery, complete with YT logo, on a Leyland Leopard/Willowbrook at Wombwell in 1972.

Left: **And then there were 49.** The Colchester Borough Transport fleet includes a number of ECW-bodied Leyland Atlanteans, including 1975 examples with this unusual style of body.

I Was There. The best ride of them all — Moulton's eight-wheeler photographed in 1974.

Driving Down Under. Two traditional Sydney-style double-deckers against the background of Sydney's middle harbour in 1971. A 1949 AEC Regent with Com.Eng. body accompanies a 1948 Leyland Titan OPD2/Clyde.

Twixt Tyne and Wear. In central Newcastle in 1978, two Tyne & Wear PTE vehicles — a Metropolitan and an Alexander-bodied Leyland Atlantean PDR2/1.

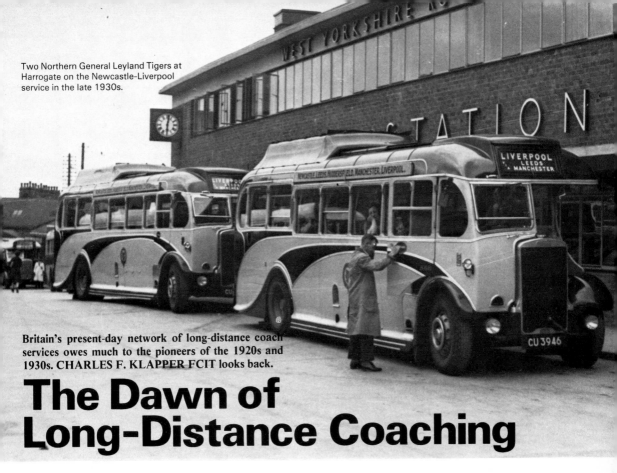

Two Northern General Leyland Tigers at Harrogate on the Newcastle-Liverpool service in the late 1930s.

Britain's present-day network of long-distance coach services owes much to the pioneers of the 1920s and 1930s. CHARLES F. KLAPPER FCIT looks back.

The Dawn of Long-Distance Coaching

Like many other aspects of mechanised road transport, long-distance coach operation fell victim to a false start, partly through over-confidence. The Vanguard buses started off in London full of rather brash ideas; that they could run the horse buses off the road by getting there quicker and charging roughly half the fare. Another idea of the early motor bus proprietors was that they could enlarge the radius of operation considerably — the General had a limitation of radius of operation to 15 miles from Charing Cross written into articles of association — and so on 30 August 1905 a daily Vanguard service was begun from Northumberland Avenue to Brighton, and was continued throughout the winter. Ironically, no trouble was experienced with the operation of a long-distance service over 50 miles, but disaster sought out a similar Milnes-Daimler bus hired by a private party of tradesmen following the same route from Orpington.

Quite properly the driver endeavoured to change down to descend Handcross Hill at a decorous speed, and in doing so he unfortunately disrupted the crash gearbox, so that there was no longer any effective connection between the transmission brake and the rear wheels. The bus began to gather speed and, again

quite properly, the driver endeavoured to slow the vehicle by rubbing the wheels against the roadside verge, where there was a high bank. This may have had some effect, but unfortunately the bus, by now going quite fast, struck a stout overhanging bough, which swept the passengers off the top deck and swung the bus into the roadside undergrowth. Of the passengers 10 died and many were injured; long-distance operation of any sort fell into disrepute and many years later a failure in the motor business was attributed to the dampening effect of the Handcross Hill accident.

Seven years elapsed before a revival in the long-distance field, but by 1913 several operators felt they had enough experience and had put on cruises for holiday passengers. In 1917 Chapman's of Eastbourne began a twice-weekly coach service from their home town to the Grosvenor Hotel in London and, as petrol was restricted at the time, town gas was provided in a balloon carried on a tray above the passenger seats. I did not see anything of the London excursion but Chapman's were very busy round Eastbourne, running trips to, inter alia, Pevensey Castle, where I well remember seeing a coal-gas standpipe for filling the balloons, and there were no doubt others. Ill-considered industrial troubles on the railways gave a considerable boost to road transport — the railway strike of 1919 gave an opportunity for the Mersea Island Bus Company to put on a twice-daily service to London and I was delighted to see the greenish-yellow open-top Straker-Squire bus still in the livery it had operated for Allen in 1916 in the Bow Road one afternoon on my way home from school and bearing the extreme destination 'West Mersea' — a 50-mile contrast from the Liverpool Street-West Kilburn service Allen had operated in London.

A certain stubborn refusal by the railways to provide adequate rolling stock contributed to the situation and Len Turnham, who was running a coach service between Victoria and Brighton with a 28-seat AEC by this time, gathered quite a bit of business by going along the queue of waiting passengers at the Victoria railway booking office offering seats at 10s 6d (52½p) single and £1 return. Pressure from stranded holiday-makers caused the East Kent Road Car Company to put on emergency services from Kent Coast resorts to London in 1919, and Southdown ran a service of coaches from Brighton to London as a temporary expedient. Further along the South Coast Bournemouth & District, as it was then known, was

unable to do anything as it had made an agreement that what became known as Hants & Dorset should hand over all long-distance business to Elliott Brothers (Bournemouth) Limited which since 1908, had been operating motor vehicles still labelled 'Royal Blue' and which had been in business with horse vehicles since 1880. This later proved a snag, because when the Southern Railway wanted a road service from London it had to be provided by Greyhound Motors of Bristol for some time instead of Elliotts whose agreement of 1921 prohibited Hants & Dorset from operating freely.

In 1920 Len Turnham began an Eastbourne service and Pickfords began to operate coaches to Brighton, Eastbourne and Hastings. To the last-named resort Timpson began a regular service from Plumstead. From New Cross the MT Company began a Margate service on 29 May 1920, a priority of which Rowand Harker, the first traffic commissioner took no notice when licences were applied for in 1931, under the Road Traffic Act 1930. Rowand Harker was rather a harsh man, imbued with an idea of doing something to protect existing bus and coach operators and the railways. In this case his sympathies were lavished upon the number of unremunerative rural services East Kent had to maintain. A rather roundabout

Left: The wrecked Vanguard Milnes-Daimler after the Handcross Hill accident which put back long-distance coaching for a decade.

Above: Coach operators' publicity for day trips — a tantalising row of East Kent advertising boards.

Woolwich, New Cross and Southend service was run from 10 July 1920 by Westcliff-on-Sea Charabanc Company. The coach was really popularised by a man out of the film industry, George Berthold Samuelson, who formed the Samuelson Transport Co Ltd with £5,000 of initial publicity.

The company was incorporated on 14 April and began trading on 7 May 1921. Only six coaches were owned at that stage, the rest of the fleet to serve all resorts between Yarmouth and Portsmouth being hired. A free collection and delivery service for luggage was provided in addition. At the end of the season 99 coaches (56 coaches under hire-purchase) and 23 luggage vans were in operation. Because 83 of the coaches were subject at that time to a 12mph speed limit, 16 more coaches with 14 seats, which could operate under the then regulations at 20mph, were obtained and with them 'first class express services' were begun on 1 July 1921 to such places as Bath, Lynton and Ilfracombe, Dawlish and Teignmouth, Newton Abbot and Torquay, and Stratford-on-Avon, Rhyl, Colwyn Bay and Llandudno. Other services advertised were Matlock and Buxton and Harrogate, but apparently these never came into operation.

Samuelson's later emerged as a subsidiary of London Coastal Coaches, an idea suggested in 1920 by Shirley James of Pickford's as London & Coastal Motor Coach Services. The London control was at first in the hands of Pickfords, but Turnham & Co took it over in 1921 and established a central control point and charting room at 7b Lower Belgrave Street; the principle of not allocating particular seats to particular travellers was accepted early on and throughout the standards have been of the highest class. One advantage obtained by the pooling system is that vehicles are always assured of mechanical maintenance at their home town and of course from other operators in the pool along the way.

Traffic at London Coastal increased rapidly, and this resulted in the partners forming a separate company capable of entering into contracts in its own name. This was incorporated on 30 April 1925. A site for a station which would not be so obstructive to traffic as Lower Belgrave Street was then sought and obtained in the shape of a plot put on one side for a Western Generating Station for the LCC Tramway an idea given up in 1920 when it became quite clear that tramways along West End thoroughfares, such as Park Lane, Kings Road and Edgware Road, were never going to see authorisation. Removal of the terminal work of London Coastal to Lupus Street coach station solved many of the problems of the police in connection with the termination of coaches in the central area, and Turnham took over the management.

Lupus Street coach station opened on 1 April 1928; the limitations of the site soon became apparent and plans for a covered station were put in hand. This was opened on 10 March 1932 by Percy J. Pybus, Minister of Transport at the time, and it secured an unprecedented audience of important figures in the bus and coach industry, including representatives of all the railway-associated companies and some minor ones, among which was the diminutive West London Coaches of Sutherland Avenue, Maida Vale, one-time operator of a London-Aylesbury service.

Some of the larger London independent bus owners wanted to continue in business after the London Passenger Transport Board Act had come into operation and made plans for continuance accordingly. The City Motor Omnibus Co Ltd purchased New Empress Saloons, with a London to Southend coach service, on 20 November 1928. City also bought operators round Brentwood (one for £7,500 Mallender told me) and converted the fleet on the Southend service of Leyland Lion coaches to Dorman diesel engines, reducing the fuel consumption to 14mpg. Birch Brothers Ltd, for similar reasons, developed a London-Rushden service. The single coach of H. J. Barnett was acquired in January 1929 and the fleet of Beaumont Safeway on the London-Bedford service in September 1932. Ten small operators were also bought in rural Hertfordshire and Bedfordshire. Premier, an erstwhile London independent, reached out as far as Aylesbury, where it rechristened Young's Aylesbury Bus Company 'Aylesbury Line'. Westminster, which in London operated the biggest bus in London, a 64-seat Sunbeam Sikh, decided to operate to Cambridge with a Gilford and a Dennis, both of which had clerestory roofs. Many destinations in East Anglia were tried but none for long. By July 1933 Westminster had had enough and sold its 23 Dennis and Gilfords vehicles to Thos Tilling Ltd, by which they were passed on 1 October 1933 to the Eastern Counties Omnibus Co Ltd.

Gray was another London independent with coach-operating ideas; its first coach was an AEC obtained in 1920; six years later a Garford (converted into a Gilford) was on the books and on 12 March 1928 two London to Oxford (via Maidenhead and Henley and via Uxbridge and Stokenchurch) services were begun. The London starting point was Bush House, Aldwych, also starting point for services to Paignton, Exeter, Torquay and Margate. The Gray London bus fleet was allowed to run down and when arrangements were made for a take-over by the LGOC; K-type General buses had to be brought in six days earlier than intended, on 6 March 1930.

This flurry of regular long-distance coach services every day of the week was attributable to the inauguration by Greyhound of Bristol, a company which had been in the coach business since March 1920 when it was founded by Toogood & Bennett, of a London to Bristol service on 11 February 1925. The London starting point was the Clarendon Hotel in Hammersmith Broadway, where one waited uncertain as to how long the police would allow the coach to stand. The original vehicles were Dennis on 'cushion' tyres. The Greyhound management had not yet been able to persuade itself of the merits of the giant pneumatic and I remember vividly the rattle set up by the cushion tyres as we ran over the rough macadam in Savernake Forest. In 1926 a repeat trip, with pneumatic tyres on an AEC coach, was much smoother, but then the road surface was better. As sequel to the first trip we toured the Mendip Country from Bath, in an open coach with a cape cart hood and side curtains which the driver (with the aid of the passengers) erected at each heavy rainstorm. Fed up with this my father decided to leave the tour at Shepton Mallet where we transferred to the Somerset & Dorset Joint Railway and listened to a 2-8-0 storming to Masbury Summit up the 1 in 50 banks. By changing at Templecombe (something I had always wanted to do) we reached Salisbury for the night and spent some time next day riding to Winchester on the Hants & Dorset and thence by Aldershot & District (known more recently as Alder Valley) to Guildford whence we achieved London by the East Surrey. On this trip electric headlights (as opposed to the acetylene headlights for so long standard on the London bus) seemed to come into their own, making all the countryside a fairyland. In 1926 we came back to London by service bus via Wickwar, Stow-on-the-Wold, Oxford and Aylesbury, the last part of the journey being on one of the Aylesbury Motor Bus Company's elderly Daimlers before we got into the London Underground area at Watford.

Another delightful occasion was created by the genial John Sword, at that time the ex-baker and principal of Midland Bus Services of Airdrie and very shortly to organise Western SMT for the Scottish Motor Traction Company. He had taken delivery of the first two diesel coaches on AEC Regal chassis and synchronised their delivery on 10 March 1932 with running them all the way from the new London Coastal terminal to Glasgow. For convenience a party of journalists was invited to cover the journey, changing over to the Glasgow-London coach at roughly half-way, that is to say at Boroughbridge, 206

Side by side at Southampton, a 1935 Western National Bristol
JJW/MCW from Devon and a 1937 Midland Red SLR from
Birmingham.

miles from London. The enhanced power available
from the diesel engine was at once apparent and in fact
the first time the driver had to make a gear change
other than for acceleration purpose was in the tortuous
streets of Stamford (well known as a 'shoulder-
breaker') 92 miles from London. The 130hp oil engine
revealed itself as capable of sustained acceleration in
top gear from traffic blocks and, because the traffic
commissioners were very interested in speeds at that
time, of keeping under 30mph, a typical stage being
the seven miles to Biggleswade from Baldock at
29mph and the 26 miles from Wetherby at 26.5mph.
The scheduled speed for the service at that time was
26.5mph except in the Northern traffic area where it
was 25mph.

Services which did not enter London had become of
some importance earlier. George Samuel Dicks, the
pioneer of service numbers, retired to Brighton in 1918
and as Vanguard Motor Conveyance Services, entered
the excursion business. In 1921 he began a Brighton-
Ashford-Margate route and the following year he was
tangled with the Cambrian group and the venture soon
afterwards faded out. Also in 1921, the Birmingham &
Midland Motor Omnibus Co Ltd (which now calls

itself Midland Red) began a Weston-super-Mare
service from Birmingham on 9 May and one to
Llandudno on 16 June.

Very soon every main road of importance in the
country had achieved its own coach service and
attempts were made at establishing other coach
stations, notably in the Kings Cross neighbourhood,
but none has achieved the prestige of London Coastal,
or as it has been renamed recently, National Travel
(South East), a less-than-catchy name which in the
long run will probably he reflected in lower receipts.

No European country has a better developed coach
and bus network than Great Britain and this is in part
due to the enlightened facility of the Road Traffic Act
of 1930 which made special provision for coach fares
(which did not exist in 1925 when we made our Bristol
trip and there were stage fares over various sections of
route). The spread of education, which may be
attributed to coach travel, is debatable, but in 1925
downright ignorance existed, as instanced by the
elderly gentleman who, passing Silbury Hill, which we
knew to be an ancient British earthwork, declared, that
'there is a volcano surely'.

A notable coach undertaking, dating from the days

of horse traction, was Elliott Brothers (Bournemouth) Ltd which operated as Royal Blue services. Thomas Elliott began operating horse coaches in 1880 and his sons turned over to motors in 1908. Daringly, tours of up to 100 miles in length were operated almost immediately. From 1922 Daimler 45hp vehicles with sleeve-valve engines were used on the London-Bournemouth express service and although known to be heavy on oil these were smooth runners and still in service a decade later. From March 1928 the London-Basingstoke-Southampton-Bournemouth service ran twice daily; the following season a route to Exeter and Torquay was introduced, and very quickly most of the main roads to the south-west were being served and the principal service to Bournemouth was being operated 10 times daily. The Tilling group secured control of Royal Blue in November 1934 and the long-distance services were subsequently transferred to the Western and Southern National companies.

The level of coach fares was a subject that was a bone of contention in the traffic courts despite the railway ownership of about 50% of the coach business from 1929 onwards, although the railways soon gave up the struggle.

Northern main roads were supplied with coach services mainly during 1928 and 1929, although the Leeds-London service of the South Yorkshire Motor Company was in full blast by September 1926. At first the coaches competed not only with the railways but with coastal shipping. The great name on the Great North Road in 1927 was Orange; its service, begun once weekly on 12 June 1927, was twice weekly by 23 June and daily from 10 October. Armstrong's Majestic Saloon Motor Coach Service became daily from 9 October and was extended to Edinburgh and Glasgow from 23 March 1931. Back in 1927 the Leeds-Newcastle Omnibus Co Ltd began operating on 3 August. The large associated bus companies formed pools which shared administrative expenses between operators, enabled more lavish expenditure on publicity and mutual security in cases of breakdown or accident.

West Yorkshire was the pioneer, beginning in July 1929 between Harrogate and London and in August between Birmingham and Harrogate. From July 1930 the Yorkshire Services pool was begun with Great North Road services between London and Harrogate; Bradford and London; Keighley and Birmingham via Sheffield; Harrogate and Birmingham via Nottingham. East Yorkshire began in July 1929 from Scarborough to Birmingham and joined the pool in 1931; the pool operators also obtained licences for such previous operations of East Yorkshire as Scarborough-Birmingham and Scarborough-London. In October 1934 the pool purchased Hale Garage and Coachways Ltd.

Northern General Transport Co Ltd inaugurated what came to be known as the Limited Stop Pool on 1 May 1928. At first it was a service of charabancs, licensed by the police authorities at Newcastle, Manchester and Liverpool; for an experiment it was operated in the following winter, and the results being profitable an increased service was planned to begin on 15 May 1929. The participants were Northern General, West Yorkshire, Woollen District and North Western companies and the headway was at first every two hours. Subsequently an extension was made on some journeys via Altrincham to Liverpool; when a Hull-Manchester service was begun by East Yorkshire this became part of the pool from February 1930. Two years later Lancashire United joined the pool and the Manchester-Liverpool service became hourly. On 18 October 1933 Tyne & Mersey Services (Newcastle-Bradford-Liverpool) was purchased and the Newcastle-Leeds section of the Fawdon Bus Company was taken over. On 31 August 1932 Redwing Safety Services' route between Leeds and Middlesbrough (with a Redcar summer extension) was taken over by West Yorkshire and United Automobile Services but permission to add United Automobile Services to the pool was held up by the Traffic Comissions, who did not view economies in working the same way as operators did. Leeds-Hull was withdrawn on 9 December 1934 and East Yorkshire ceased to be a pool member; however, on 21 October 1934 the Commissioners gave their blessing to the joining of the pool by United. By 1939 there was an hourly frequency between Liverpool and Leeds and on Saturdays from Leeds to Newcastle.

A scheme of co-ordination usually known as the Blackpool picture was brought about by the traffic commissioners in 1932 and 1934 and provided for co-ordination on a rota basis of various minor operators, with one company as clearing house and arrangements for joint publicity.

The biggest co-ordination scheme among coach operators was undoubtedly that centred on Cheltenham, sometimes termed in the popular press 'the Clapham Junction of the coachways'. In the early 1920s G. Reading began a garage and motor coach undertaking at Charlton Kings and Cheltenham which he named 'Black & White Luxury Coaches' and on 12 April 1928 he formed it into a limited company. Two years later the capital of the company was jointly acquired by Birmingham & Midland Motor Omnibus Co Ltd, Bristol Tramways & Carriage Co Ltd and City of Oxford Motor Services Ltd, and H. R. Lapper became general manager. His brother, L. B. Lapper, was well known in railway enthusiast circles as a joint founder of the Railway Correspondence and Travel

A United Counties Bristol J05G on the Kettering-Cheltenham service, at Stow-on-the-Wold.

A City Coach 1937 Leyland Tiger TS7D on the Kentish Town-Southend service which was purchased from New Empress.

Society but took no part in coach operation. In 1933 Black & White and the company's St Margarets Coach Station in Cheltenham was selected to be the focal point of services to Wales and the West of England and the first stage with services of Black & White, Birmingham & Midland, Greyhound, and Red & White began meeting on 19 March 1934 twice a day, once about the lunch interval and the other at tea-time; during these periods passengers exchanged vehicles and could obtain a meal. In May the second stage was completed with the addition of services of Elliott Brothers of Bournemouth (Royal Blue), Ribble, and United Counties and publicity using the name Associated Motorways appeared from 1 July 1934.

Many thought that sleeping-car services on rail could be equalled by road, but Chergwin (known on the music halls as the White Kaffir) found his service between London and Manchester was ruined by the laundry bills. Many would-be operators of restaurant facilities (usually carried out on the upper decks of double-deck vehicles) have found that it is difficult to make refreshments pay and it is best to leave passengers to make their own arrangements at stops. Built-in lavatory arrangements are very seldom provided on coaches.

For many years charting was done on a first-come-first-served basis but of recent years carousel methods have been used for booking of excursion traffic. Factors making a big difference to coach operation of recent years are: the increased mileage of special roads for motor vehicles (including motorways); the increased number of bypasses; and the relaxation of speed limits (from 12mph at the beginning of the motor era to 70mph on motorways today). In 1932 the London-Glasgow time was 16hr 23min; today it is 11hr by A roads and $8\frac{1}{2}$ by the motorways. The Hammersmith-Bristol service which in 1925 took eight hours now occupies 3hr 25min by A roads or $2\frac{1}{2}$ hr by motorway and, of course, has the extra mileage represented by Hammersmith to London Coastal Coaches terminal to traverse.

A peaceful scene in Tudor Square, Dalton-in-Furness, from a
1935 postcard. This bus is a Ribble 1930 Leyland Lion LT2 with
30-seat Leyland body.

Buses to the fore in Market Place, Stockton, in 1933, featuring
three Stockton Corporation vehicles (*left to right*) a Leyland TD1,
Daimler CP6 and Leyland Lioness.

Odd Bods

A selection of some of the more unusual coach bodies which were produced in the 1960s.

Right: The Burlingham Seagull 70 body was less successful than the classic 1950 Seagull. This Eastern Scottish AEC Reliance 34-seat coach was built in 1961, the year after the Burlingham business was acquired by Duple.

Below: The Burlingham coachworks at Blackpool continued as Duple (Northern) and for 1963 the Firefly body was introduced, suitable for Ford Trader, Albion Victor, or, as seen here, Bedford SB.

Above: Another product of the Burlingham works, the Duple Continental of 1961, on one of the very first 36ft AEC Reliance chassis.

Below: This attractive coach was the solitary Duple Astrocoach body, on AEC Reliance chassis. The high, curved windows anticipated later trends.

The Weymann Castilian was basically a modernised and lengthened Fanfare, and was unique to Southdown. This was a 1963 Castillian-bodied Leyland Leopard.

Weymann tried to break into the lightweight coach market in 1962 with the Topaz and Amethyst bodies for Bedford SB and VAL chassis. This was the Amethyst prototype, on Bedford VAL14 chassis; the body, perhaps not surprisingly, did not prove popular.

The MCW Metropolitan coach body (*above*) was successful visually, but sales were disappointing. It was introduced in 1967, and the prototype was rebuilt from the one-off Athena (*right*) which appeared in the demonstration park at the 1966 Commercial Motor Show, on Bedford VAM chassis.

Below: MCW's Topaz II, introduced in 1965, enjoyed a limited success. This example on Bedford VAL14 was owned by Clarke's of London.

The crisply-styled Park Royal Royalist was introduced in 1967. It was originally offered on Albion's rear-engined Viking VK43L chassis — a real Leyland Group effort. The intention was to offer the Royalist on Bedford and Ford chassis in 1968, but in the event only a limited number of Vikings was produced.

The unusual, and slightly fussy rear end of the Royalist, incorporating grilles for the Viking engine.

A real oddity — not, as it proclaims, a Mercedes-Benz, but a Leyland Olympic sub-frame with a Van Hool body. It started life as one of the famous Leyland/MCW Olympics for Cuba; in 1964, the ship carrying 42 Olympics from Britain sank in the Thames, and this was one of two salvaged buses bought by Smiths of Wigan. They received new integral Van Hool 44-seat bodies, and although still left-hand drive, they were registered in Britain.

Driving Down Under

Some random recollections of the enjoyment — and occasional discomfort — of working on the buses in Melbourne, Sydney and Queensland, by ROBERT GRIEVES.

I can't really recall whether it was the attraction of a sunny climate, higher wages or a generally jaded attitude towards life in Britain, probably aggravated by the demise of David MacBrayne's bus services where I was a driver at the time. Whatever the reason, an advert for tram conductors placed in a Sunday paper by the imposingly named Melbourne and Metropolitan Tramways Board spurred me into finally making up my mind to go to Australia. The M&MTB held local interviews at various centres throughout Britain and also made the necessary travel arrangements. Consequently in April 1970 I joined the liner *Fairstar* at Southampton for what was surely the best travel bargain possible — Australia for £10, under the assisted passage scheme.

On arrival at Melbourne, the Board had a reception vehicle waiting on the quay to meet the 20 or so new recruits from the UK. When I saw it I got quite excited and considered it was very fortunate that they had sent what surely must be one of their last remaining half-cab AEC Regals. I was soon to discover that this type made up a large proportion of the fleet, and to drive them daily in service through Melbourne's heavy traffic required a great deal of enthusiasm!

All the new 'pommy' recruits were assigned to various depots throughout the city. I worked initially as a tram conductor at Malvern depot but quickly transferred to North Fitzroy, as I preferred to be on the buses. This was the only dual Tram/bus depot in the system; it also housed the central bus workshops. All the buses here were single-deckers of AEC Regal Mk III and Mk IV types, as the only double-deckers in the fleet had been replaced some years before by trams! Soon I passed through the driving school on the Leyland Tiger OPS1 kept for that purpose, and was available for driving shifts as well as bus and tram conducting. When spare, it was possible to conduct a tram, a bus and drive a bus, both crew and one-man operated, all during the same shift!

After a few months, a vacancy arose on the one-man drivers' roster and so my conducting days ended. Basically North Fitzroy operated only two OMO routes; from the city to West Heidelberg and from Clifton Hill to Elsternwick. The latter was solely worked by the Regal IIIs, designed in my opinion to turn all tall drivers into hunchbacks since the driving seats had poor adjustment and the low destination box tended to obscure one's view unless a stooping posture

Left: Robert Grieves between two Brisbane buses, the first of 98 Volvo B59s, and one of 340 Leyland Panthers.

Below: A former Tyne & Wear PTE Weymann-bodied Atlantean throws up the dust in its new life with Argent's Bus Service, Kempsey NSW, in 1976.

was adopted. Add to this the discomfort of turning round to issue tickets and straining to hear the fare requested above the throb of the engine and one can immediately sympathise with the driver. At least we had ticket machines, which incidentally were ex-London Transport Gibsons, which was an improvement on the bus and tram conductors, who carried a huge leather wallet holding many values of paper tear-off tickets.

A shift on West Heidelberg with a semi-automatic Regal IV was therefore regarded as generally more desirable than Elsternwick with a pre-select Mk III. Heavy steering on the former was the major complaint, especially if carrying a full load, since the extra weight on the front overhang made quite a difference. These buses, and the one-man operated Mk IIIs, had their bodies cut short immediately behind the rear axle, since the union would only agree to a maximum of 31 seats in OMO vehicles. The point which struck me as rather self-defeating, however, was that there was no limit on standing passengers!

My spare time in Melbourne was often spent in travelling on some of the many interesting buses, trams and trains within easy reach. Melbourne's host of independent bus operators at that time used some most unusual vehicles, ranging from early American Reos to modern Japanese Hinos. Aptly named Victorian Railways still served some suburban lines

with electric trains built in Victoria's reign, while interesting excursions by electric, diesel, and occasionally steam trains could also be made.

A little farther afield, a day trip could be made to the northern Victorian one-time gold mining centres of Ballarat and Bendigo to enjoy their delightful tramway systems, both of which transmitted that leisurely feeling of having all the time in the world. Alas, these have since been abandoned, but thanks to the dedication of enthusiast societies have been saved, at least in part, and so still give pleasure to those who visit these towns.

Hopefully some enthusiast will also save one of those hardy half-cab Regals which served Melbourne so well for so long. They were not fitted with trafficators, by the way, but carried a mechanical hand at the end of a metal arm. This was pushed through the side of the cab when intending to stop, and it emerged in an upright position. Before turning right, by depressing a catch when pushing out the arm, it released the hand in an outstretched position. Tail lights could not be turned on from the cab, but only from a switch at the rear exterior of the bus. Needless to say, children playing at terminal points were also aware of this switch! I believe that, in the Regal IIIs which remain, these anachronisms have at long last been replaced by flashers and cab-controlled tail lights.

After a year in Melbourne I began to hanker after

pastures new, and a week-end visit to Sydney during which I had seen real live Albion Venturers quickly decided my choice of destination.

By far the greater part of Sydney was served by the routes of the New South Wales Department of Government Transport (now the Public Transport Commission of NSW). It was at the Burwood depot I started as a driver/conductor. Burwood was hard work, serving routes along the busy Parramatta Road, one of the main arteries out to the west. The buses at that time were mainly Leyland Titan OPD2s with that individual style of bodywork characteristic of Sydney deckers. Very nice to drive — Sydney's buses were generally well maintained — but a personal criticism was their inadequate driving mirrors which were small squares of flat glass and which, especially in thick traffic, left blind spots.

Before long, I transferred to North Sydney depot, which with 40 buses was one of the smallest in the system, although it had been much larger in the days of the trams, which were finally withdrawn in 1961. All buses here were single-deckers, including 43-seat Leyland Worldmasters and 31-seat AEC Regal IIIs and Leyland Tiger OPS2s. These 31-seaters were used on North Sydney's several wharf runs, which connected with the harbour ferries at a variety of north shore suburbs and ran on generally fairly short routes to the local shopping centres. The change from Burwood was almost like going on holiday. In fact, very often I would take advantage of the waiting time at a harbour side terminal point in the heat of a Sydney summer to freshen up by having a paddle!

A rather unusual feature of roster operations in Sydney was that driver/conductors, until they were attached to a duty cycle of their own, could be loaned out to other depots throughout the system. Thus from my own depot I travelled all over Sydney, and so sampled most types of bus in operation.

In 1970 new Leyland Atlanteans were introduced and these replaced the remaining elderly Albion Venturers at Brookvale depot on the north side of the city. The majority of these, however, found new homes with private operators throughout New South Wales, and continued in service for several years — a few are still running.

The Venturers naturally reminded me of the once large fleet operated back home in Glasgow. Indeed Sydney's fleet of Albions was second only in size to that of Glasgow. Bodywork, to the standard DGT design was by a variety of builders, including batches by Clyde Engineering of Sydney. These Clyde-built Albions seemed to me particularly appropriate in their nomenclature, and brought out my deepest feelings of nostalgia, akin to other expatriates hearing the bagpipes.

The aforementioned Atlanteans carried bodies again distinctive to Sydney, which were not contenders for any design award, even incorporating the mechanical 'stop warning', hand initially, as earlier described. A lengthy strike was caused by plans to operate them as one-man buses, which did not eventuate due to union opposition. For Atlanteans their passenger capacity was small, since with 66 seated and five standing the total was only 71, as opposed to a Leyland Leopard with 42 plus 27 giving 69. All things considered, they were not the success hoped for and their final numbers were limited.

As in Melbourne, my off-duty hours were often spent on trips elsewhere in the state, occasionally travelling long distances by British standards to visit country centres with transport interest. Glen Innes, for instance, in northern NSW is the home of one of the last of a once very popular type of bus in rural Australia. In that very Scottish-sounding town in the area of the state paradoxically known as New England lived a Ford V8 'side loader' of 1948 which worked the passenger and mail run to Inverell. The elderly owners also had three other similar examples which were retained for spares. Like charabancs of the 1920s, they had a door to each row of seats. When neither the number of passengers nor weight of mail justified the use of the 'big' bus, then an almost equally elderly Holden saloon car would tow a small trailer over the route.

Many interesting vehicles could be found in operation with independents around Sydney, and it was an easy matter to visit such firms on days off.

How many enthusiasts have wondered whatever happened to those Cuban-bound Leyland-MCW Olympics which were deck cargo aboard a ship which sank while leaving the Thames some years ago? It may be recalled that a fleet of them sailed for that Caribbean island despite a great deal of controversy concerning the morals involved over Britain trading with the Castro regime.

The buses were eventually salvaged and bought by English dealers, where Mr John Bosnjak of the Parramatta Bus Co, to the west of Sydney found them while over on a business trip. Nine of them were shipped to Australia where, owing to the poor condition of their bodies, eight were rebodied locally by CVI. One, however, was found to be in sufficiently good order to operate with its original body, albeit after conversion to left-hand doors and right-hand driving position.

My next move was again north, when I headed over the border from NSW into Queensland where I worked first for the now defunct Sunnybank Bus Service of Acacia Ridge, just to the south of Brisbane, capital city of the state. Sunnybank operated an

Typical of the Melbourne trams driven by the author on his arrival in Australia. Three of the W2 class — built from 1923 onwards, and still in service in large numbers — seen in 1970 in St Kilda Road with the Shrine of Remembrance in the background.

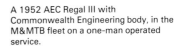

A 1952 AEC Regal III with Commonwealth Engineering body, in the M&MTB fleet on a one-man operated service.

One of the older privately-owned buses still operating in Melbourne in the early 1970s was this Reo of Royena Motors, with locally-built Grummet body.

109

The author's favourite Sydney buses were the Albions. Bus 1910, with Commonwealth Engineering body, was a Venturer of 1947 vintage, seen here leaning into a corner at North Ryde.

assortment of interesting buses, both new and second-hand, each of which had its own eccentricities calling for various driving techniques. The variety of vehicles included some uncommon and some completely unknown in UK fleets. There was an AEC Ranger for example, a Mack, a White, a couple of Leyland Comets, and Albions were well represented with a Valkyrie, an Aberdonian, two Clydesdales and several Vikings. Despite being a small independent operator, Sunnybank used Almex ticket machines unlike the Brisbane municipal fleet and even the NSW Department of Government Transport — Australia's largest bus operator, who both remained faithful to the tear-off, pre-printed paper ticket system.

After Sunnybank, I later drove for Brisbane City Council Transport Department. At this stage may I answer a question which must be in the minds of many people, since I am often asked 'How on earth did you find your way driving a bus around strange cities on the other side of the world?' Quite simply a city in Australia is no stranger than any in Britain which is not one's own. I would find driving for the first time in Birmingham or London equally as hard as I did in Melbourne or Sydney. Admittedly there are some minor difference in road traffic rules, but traffic drives on the left as in this country so basic common sense is

the main requirement in my view. On one-man operated routes there is little excuse for taking a wrong turning, since a passenger will always keep you right — or left as the case may be!

On school buses, which invariably wander around all sorts of unlikely places not on on normal routes, a pupil will often offer to show you where to go without being asked. Caution should be exercised on the way to school in the morning, as often the kids delight in directing unsuspecting drivers *away* from the school, whereas in the afternoon one could be fairly certain that correct directions would be given as most pupils were then eager to return home.

The main part of Brisbane's fleet consisted of 340 Leyland Panthers — the largest fleet of Panthers in the world. These were delivered to replace the city's trams in 1968-9. Despite the fact that Panthers never found great favour in Britain, Brisbane's examples led a relatively trouble-free existence, and were popular with drivers and passengers alike.

Queensland's warmth was the reason for Brisbane's bus fleet being fitted with cane driving seats, which I believe was unique in Australia, if not the world. Perhaps not the most comfortable of seats on a long shift, but at least one did not stick to them.

How enjoyable it was to set off to work, even at

Left: A Brisbane AEC Regal III of 1949 with Hedges body.
Above: One of Sydney's Atlanteans, with Pressed Metal Corporation body.

some unearthly hour in the early morning, wearing merely a pair of shorts and a short-sleeved shirt. Such was my uniform in sub-tropical Brisbane and also in Sydney, and I believe even staid Victorian Melbourne has now introduced shorts for summer wear. One has a definite feeling of increased freedom when thus attired, rather than plodding off to work in the freezing fog of a British winter, encumbered by heavy jacket and overcoat. I can also vouch for the fact that a comfortably warm climate encourages one to perform the day's duty in a more relaxed and contented frame of mind.

Passengers, inevitably, are the same on both sides of the world. The same large denomination notes are tendered on early morning runs and the same complaints are voiced regarding early, late or non-running of the bus in front, as though you had some magical control over it at well as your own.

The following is a true account of an incident which highlights one of the differences of life in Australia, and which is not liable to occur here in Britain.

It happened when I was in Brisbane and was first related to an appreciative audience in the depot canteen in extremely colourful language by one of the many 'pommy' migrant drivers. Apparently he had reason to use the convenience at one of the outer

terminal points. The dry toilet, like many others in Brisbane provided for the transport department, was a small wooden hut in a field adjacent to the terminus. My colleague was in a seated position when he caught sight of a large snake coiled in the sawdust box on the wall.

A poisonous snake? I asked with interest. Apparently George had not lingered to find out, as the small group of passengers waiting to board his bus could testify. They were greeted with the somewhat startling spectacle of a Brisbane bus driver emerging at speed from the toilet, simultaneously hastily hoisting up his trousers.

Although I am now resident in Britain once more, my thoughts often turn to Australia and the most enjoyable years I spent there.

I would certainly recommend anyone who has the opportunity to visit Australia to do so. Admittedly a lot of the former transport interest has lessened with the passage of time. It is nevertheless still a fascinating country for a great variety of all forms of transport and the enthusiast from the UK can now find many examples of former British buses 'down under' from ex-City of Oxford AEC Renowns to Selnec Leyland Panthers or AEC Merlins of the London Transport MB class.

Off to the Seaside

G. R. MILLS photographs of some of the coaches that carried Londoners to the sea at Clacton and Southend in the 1960s.

Above: At Southend's Kursaal in 1961, a smart Leyland Tiger PS2, with Harrington body, from the Grey-Green fleet.

Right: This 1955 AEC Reliance with ECW-influenced Park Royal Royalist body makes an interesting comparison with the 1967 Royalist on page 105. In the fleet of Timpson's, Catford, it is seen at Clacton in 1966.

A rare combination — Dodge S307 chassis with Strachans Pacemaker 41-seat coach body, in the Rickards, Brentford fleet against the background of the Southend Kursaal in 1964.

A bulbous Bellhouse Hartwell 35-seat coach body was fitted to this Daimler Freeline D650HS seen in Southend in the fleet of Blankley of Colsterworth, Lincs.

The contemporary, but more successful, Windover body fitted to an AEC Regal IV in the fleet of Harris, Grays at Clacton in 1962.

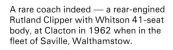

A rare coach indeed — a rear-engined Rutland Clipper with Whitson 41-seat body, at Clacton in 1962 when in the fleet of Saville, Walthamstow.

The immaculate fleet of Delaine, Bourne was a good customer of Yeates, the Loughborough coachbuilder with a weakness for the ornate. This 1960 Bedford SB was at Clacton in 1961 on hire to Eastern Counties.

Another Yeates product, this time on 1956 AEC Reliance chassis for London Co-op whose coaches were familiar at Clacton for many years.

At Southend's Kursaal in 1962, an interesting 1950 Bedford OB with a Baico chassis extension to give 33 seats in the Plaxton body. It was owned by Britchford, of Yaxley, Hunts.

This 1950 Dennis Lancet III sported a 1960 Thurgood 37-seat body when photographed at the Kursaal in 1966, in the smart two blue of Horseshoe of Tottenham.

The first Passenger Transport Executives took over just ten years ago. G. COXON looks at the first decade of the Tyne & Wear PTE.

Twixt Tyne and Wear

By far the smallest and most viable of the eight passenger transport executives operating today is Tyne & Wear PTE. It was one of the four original PTEs devised in the 1960s by Transport Minister Barbara Castle, although at that time it covered only the Tyneside area. On 1 April 1969, the Tyneside passenger transport authority was formed, and on 1 January, 1970 the passenger transport executive began operations of the former Newcastle and South Shields Corporations. At that time both fleets consisted mainly of double-deckers, Newcastle with 350 plus two single-deckers, all painted in cadmium yellow and white with maroon wheels and beadings; South Shields had 82 double-deckers and five single-deckers painted blue and primrose.

Unlike other PTEs which had decided to introduce a brand new livery for their bus fleets, Tyneside PTE adopted the former Newcastle livery and quickly applied it to the South Shields buses. A new symbol was introduced, representing the joining together of the two

undertakings with the river Tyne dividing them. This replaced the Corporation's own fleetnames and coat-of-arms.

Under the terms set out in the 1968 Transport Act, the PTE had to undertake to improve the efficiency and fully integrate the transport system within its operating boundary, which would bring maximum benefit to the travelling public. Included in these proposals was the integration of the ferry service across the river Tyne and most of the local rail services, already running at a loss and being subsidised by Government.

Surrounding the Tyneside area, as well as operating within the PTE area, were the bus services operated by two subsidiary companies of the National Bus Company, United and Northern General, including the Northern subsidiaries Sunderland District, Wakefields, Tyneside, Tynemouth, Gateshead and Venture. Already co-ordination had been struck between the Gateshead buses and the former Newcastle Corporation, as many of the cross-

Tyne services were operated on a share basis. This co-ordination was to be extended and in March 1971 a joint body was set up comprising of three PTE and three NBC Members to look at the best ways of integrating the area's bus services for maximum efficiency and cost savings to the travelling public. Cost savings were quickly implemented by the introduction on 1 April 1971 of an area travel concession scheme for pensioners, blind and certain disabled people at off peak times of the day, available on PTE and NBC buses. The scheme was modified to a free travel concession in April 1973. Meanwhile, along with every other company in the land, the PTE continued its policy of extending its one-man operation, and to cater for the increase in OMO at South Shields, Leyland Atlanteans were transferred from Newcastle to replace ageing back-loading Guy double-deckers. South Shields also had a batch of Daimler back-loaders which were retained for peak-time operations. It is interesting to note that the two original 1960 Atlanteans, one with Alexander body and the other with MCW body, were withdrawn in 1971, probably one of the first operators in the country to withdraw Atlanteans from service. The PTE's vehicle policy has been to standardise on Atlanteans and Fleetlines with bodywork by Alexander. Also delivered in 1971 were a batch of six Daimler Fleetline/Marshall single-deckers, originally ordered by South Shields for its OMO extension, and three Bedford YRQ/Duple Viceroy coaches, the PTE's first full coaches.

A new faster inter-urban express service 'Fastline', was introduced in 1972 to provide a limited stop service angled at coaxing the motorist to leave his car in the garage. The first Fastline service X62, linked Killingworth (new town) with Newcastle city centre using five new Leyland Panthers with 45-seat dual purpose Alexander bodywork; these were replaced by 10 Leyland Leopards with Willowbrook Expressway bodies in 1973. The Leyland Panthers were the last examples of this chassis to enter service on the home market.

A further move towards closer

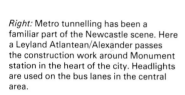

Left: Tyne & Wear PTE's Fastline services proved popular, and are operated by double-deckers like this Metropolitan, leaving Newcastle Airport for Central Station on X77.

Right: Metro tunnelling has been a familiar part of the Newcastle scene. Here a Leyland Atlantean/Alexander passes the construction work around Monument station in the heart of the city. Headlights are used on the bus lanes in the central area.

collaboration between the PTE and NBC came in July 1972 when the Gateshead fleet began to appear in a variation of the PTE livery. This was yellow and white with grey wheels and red Gateshead fleetnames, and gradually replaced the Gateshead's cream/cream livery. Eventually more of Northern's subsidiary companies, vehicles operating within the PTE area began to sport the yellow livery, although still retaining their own fleetnames. Along with many other operators, the PTE was attracted by the Leyland National, which offered a new dimension in passenger safety and driver comfort. This led to the PTE buying a batch of eight two-door Nationals in 1972.

In 1973, the PTA revealed its proposals for a rapid transit system which would revolutionise the travelling habits of everyone in the area — the Metro. This would be an electric railway system which would link the two city centres of Newcastle and Gateshead with a broad area either side of the river Tyne. The service would be operated by Metrocars, which would utilise existing local rail track as well as new track to be tunnelled under the heart of the two city centres. Many of the stations would be unmanned and tickets would be purchased from

vending machines on the station platform. The principle behind the expensive Metro system is to enable passengers to travel from north and south of the Tyne to the city centres more quickly, and to encourage the motorist to leave his car at home or outside the city centre, which would decongest the central areas of the city and provide a more efficient bus service for those living in areas outside the Metro catchment area. Full integration of PTE and NBC bus services with the Metro is also planned, with buses serving as feeders to the Metro interchange stations. Here passengers will be able to travel by bus and Metro using the same ticket. The Metro plans became reality when construction work began in 1974.

On 1 April 1973, Tyneside PTE absorbed Sunderland Corporation — a year earlier than was necessary under the provision of the 1972 Local Government Act. Ironically in the original proposals for a Tyneside PTA in the 1960s, Sunderland Corporation objected to a move by the Government to include it in the Tyneside PTA, stating that Sunderland did not consider itself part of Tyneside, but was a separate urban area. Sunderland, since 1966 under the managership of Norman

Morton, had undertaken a policy of massive one-man operation using two-door single-deck buses, and pioneered the use of the flat zonal fare system using metal tokens sold at concessionary rates. For many years the Sunderland operator traded at a loss. Sunderland Corporation operated a mixed fleet of green and cream single-deckers as well as a few Daimler Fleetline double deckers, mainly used for peak time services. Nearly every make of chassis was represented in the fleet, which was eventually repainted in the yellow and cream PTE livery. They were Marhsall-bodied Atkinsons and Leyland Panther Cubs, Strachan-bodied AEC Swifts, Leyland Panthers, and Daimler Roadliners and Metro-Cammell-bodied Bristol RELLs; there were also AEC Swifts with Marshall bodies, which were ordered by Sunderland but which were delivered to the PTE. The Sunderland-designed Strachan and Metro-Cammell bodies were of a distinctive style incorporating a flat windscreen, wide front entrance and forward-sloping window pillars.

The PTE moved into the coaching business in a big way by acquiring the old-established business of Armstrongs of Westerhope in August 1973 and its subsidiary

A Leyland Leopard/Duple
Dominant in the PTE's Armstrong Galley
coach fleet on the road to Scarborough.

Galleys' Coaches. Thirty coaches and
five double-deckers were involved
but not all the vehicles were
absorbed into the PTE fleet.
Armstrongs and Galleys were best
known for their coaching activities,
with excursion and tours licenses
held from Newcastle; however a
rural stage carriage service from
Newcastle (Newgate St.) to the
villages of Stamfordham and Matfen
in Northumberland was operated, as
well as an express service link from
Central Station to Newcastle Airport.
The PTE has maintained these
services, although with the
formation of a separate coaching
division, incorporating Armstrongs
and Galleys the services were
transferred to the bus division. The
Armstrongs' and Galleys' fleet
names have been retained on the
coaches alongside the PTE symbol.
Armstrongs coaches were painted
green and cream and Galleys in blue
and black. A predominantly Bedford
coach fleet, was absorbed into the
PTE fleet with some AEC Reliances,
and the mixed selection of double-
deckers mainly used for school
contracts were replaced by vehicles
from the PTE fleet.

With the addition of Sunderland
Corporation to the Tyneside PTE in
April 1973, a year later the newly
formed Tyne & Wear Metropolitan
County undertook responsibility for
the Tyne & Wear area and hence the
PTE was renamed Tyne & Wear PTE.
In October 1974, a revision of the
fare structure at Sunderland
heralded the end of the zonal fare
system, and service reorganisation
resulted in an increase in passengers
travelling in the Sunderland area,
now known as South Division.
Worthy of a mention is the
appearance at the 1974 Commercial
Motor Show of the prototype
Alexander T type coach body
mounted on a Leyland Leopard
chassis, seating 49 and sporting
Galley's fleet names.

With the formation of the Tyne &
Wear PTE, came a move to
completely renumber the fleet. Since
the acquisition of Sunderland,
similar fleet numbers had appeared
on Sunderland and Tyneside
vehicles, and also included in the
numbering system were Armstrongs
and Galleys coaches.

A further expansion in the
Sunderland area occurred on
1 January, 1975 when Tyne & Wear
took over the services of the
Whitburn independent operator,
Economic. Economic, jointly owned

by E. W. Wilson and G. R. Anderson
operated a busy service linking
Sunderland and South Shields along
the sea front. The service provided
an important link between Tyneside
operations and the recently-acquired
Sunderland Corporation. Although a
substantial fleet of Bedfords and
AEC Reliances was operated in dark
maroon and cream, and although
more were on the old side, they were
immaculately kept. Only two
Bedfords, a YRT/Plaxton Panorama
Express with bus seats and a
YRQ/Willowbrook bus were
transferred to the PTE, the service
now being served by newly-acquired
Leyland Nationals, one-man
operated by crews from the South
Shields depot. The service now takes
double-deckers and at weekends
during the summer season an open-
top service is provided, weather
permitting.

A further benefit to the travelling
public came on 1 May 1975 when
the travel ticket was introduced. This
enabled passengers unlimited travel
on all bus services in the Tyne &
Wear area and on the three locally-
supported rail services and the
cross-river ferry. The travel ticket
which incorporates a passport
photograph of the owner, can cover
travel for one or four weeks and is
accepted by the independent

118

Top: Tyne & Wear's latest Atlanteans with Alexander bodies have only a single door. 292, a 10 metre vehicle, is on the former Economic service from South Shields to Sunderland.

Above left: A Bristol VRT with ECW body hired by the PTE from Cardiff Transport, seen on a rail-link service at West Monkseaton.

Above: Only three Ailsa/Alexanders were bought by Tyne & Wear. They were moved to Sunderland, where they remained until withdrawal in 1978.

Left: Leaving Sunderland's enclosed central bus station, one of the PTE's Willowbrook-bodied Atlanteans.

119

operators in the area, ie W. H. Jolly, H. W. Hunter & Son, OK Motor Services and Trimdon Motor Services; only the W. H. Jolly service between South Hylton and Sunderland (Central Bus Station) run totally within the Tyne & Wear operational area.

A slightly modified fleet livery was introduced in Spring 1975 which was more noticeable on double-deckers than single-deckers. In order to save on painting costs, buses were painted yellow up to the lower deck windows and the rest of the bus cream. The first new buses in that livery were three Ailsas with Alexander 79-seat bodies, one of each going to Newcastle, South Shields and Sunderland for evaluation purposes. Their presence has not been a happy one, eventually being transferred to Sunderland where they remained until early retirement in 1978. In contrast, 10 Metropolitans followed in 1976 and made a big inpact with passengers and crews alike, and since then 140 Metropolitans have been bought, all based at Newcastle. Tyne & Wear PTE operates the second largest fleet of Metropolitans in the country, after London Transport's 164.

The outward signs of the huge tunnel construction project under the city centre was beginning to show on the surface with the appearance of cranes, pile-driving machinery, road works and temporary traffic signals in different parts of the city. If this is the price to be paid for progress, then the Newcastle public must be praised for its tolerance. Just outside the city at Middle Engine Lane, the first two prototype Metrocars were on trial on a test track, $1\frac{1}{2}$ miles long. In September 1975, Terrier Coaches, operating a daily service from Newcastle to Morpeth, folded up and the PTE took over the service. Morpeth, a market town outside the Metropolitan county boundary, has an ever-increasing population with the building of many housing estates.

A very interesting vehicle purchase took place in February 1976 when the PTE brought six 11 metre Bristol VRLL double-deck coaches from National Travel (North West). These vehicles were bought for the transfer service from Central Station to the Tyne Commission Quay, primarily for Scandinavian boat passengers. The service is operated by Northern General on behalf of the PTE and the vehicles, painted in PTE livery, are allocated to the former Tyneside depot at Wallsend and the former Tynemouth depot at Percy Main. These vehicles are ideally suited with a large baggage compartment at the rear lower deck.

During the early part of 1976 the PTE found itself seriously short of buses in the Newcastle area. Due to late deliveries of new vehicles and shortages of spare parts for existing vehicles, the choice was between refurbishing some of the older buses or to hire and buy in for a short period until new vehicles were delivered. It was to be more economical to do the latter and so in April the PTE hired in a variety of double-deckers notably Atlanteans from Bournemouth and Plymouth, Fleetlines from Southend, Leyland Titan PD3A's from Leicester, PD2s from Lothian; and it bought six AEC Regent Vs and one Leyland PD3, all ex-Leeds City Transport, from OK Motor Services, which had bought them and then decided not to use them. Also helping out were Atlanteans from the Armstrong's fleet and AEC Swifts from Sunderland depot. A delivery of ten Atlanteans with Alexander bodywork and the start of a batch of two-door Metropolitans eased the situation, and by the beginning of June things were beginning to get back to normal. Some of the AEC Regent Vs, still in two-tone green livery, except for the yellow panels either side with the PTE symbol, remained in service until late 1976. Because of the volume of work at the Alexander

coachworks Tyne & Wear PTE decided to divert an order for 30 Atlanteans to Willowbrook, to speed delivery. This did not work out this way as the batch was delayed due to problems with the tilt test. The bodies were built to the former Newcastle Corporation's own design incorporating a nearside staircase in front of the centre doors. This batch was delivered over a long period of time and some of another batch of Alexander-bodied Atlanteans were being delivered at the same time. After several accidents involving passengers and the centre exit doors the PTE decided not to order any more two-door double-deckers. It was claimed by drivers that there were blind spots and that passengers were sometimes avoiding paying fares by entering through the centre doorway.

Following the success of the Fastline services, more of these routes have been introduced, now using double-deckers. Yet another revised livery appeared on the PTE's buses in the summer of 1976, when Metropolitan and Atlantean double-deckers and a Leopard/Alexander single-decker were painted yellow and white with blue wheels and beadings. The general appearance was a great improvement on the former style. In 1977, Silver Jubilee year, the PTE introduced two

preserved vehicles into service, these being No 123 (LVK 123), an all-Leyland PD2 in the original Newcastle Corporation blue and cream livery and No 341 (NVK 341) an AEC Regent III with Northern Coachbuilders body in the yellow and cream livery of Newcastle Corporation. The two vehicles operated special service number 44 from Central Station to Gosforth Park. The same vehicles operated the same route a year later to celebrate the centenary of Newcastle Transport.

On 9 January 1978 the travelling routine of thousands of passengers was changed with the closure of the North Tyne loop rail service to allow Metro work to be carried out. The PTE retained some of its older vehicles to serve as relief vehicles during the anticipated one-year closure period. They were called Rail-Link buses and four services R1–R4 were introduced to cover the entire route from Newcastle to the coast, including places like Jesmond, Wallsend, Benton, Whitley Bay and West Monkseaton. These double-deckers are based at the United depots, Newcastle (Jesmond), Whitley Bay and Blyth, and the PTE depot at Byker.

The PTE continues to retain a modern, well-appointed fleet of buses, which gives a good

impression to the travelling public. The single-deckers inherited from Sunderland are being withdrawn and replaced by new double-deckers, while other early withdrawals have been the three Ailsa's and the L and N registered Leyland Nationals. More Atlanteans are awaited with Alexander bodies and trial batches of five each Leyland Titan and Metrobus are on order for evaluation. With the implementation of the £160 million Metro system facing some delays, the introduction of phase 1 was put back from January 1979 to September 1979, but this has coincided with delays in the expected delivery of the 90 Metro-Cammell metrocars.

The Metro system will consist of 34 miles of track and should be fully operational in 1981. The Metro has its critics, claiming that it will never be financially viable, but one thing is certain — it should benefit the commuter and relieve traffic congestion in the centres of Newcastle and Gateshead. From this angle, existing bus services will become more efficent for passengers unable to use the Metro.

If the system is efficiently operated and the fares are attractive enough, the Metro will be successful, even if it does mean a further burden to be borne by the ratepayer.

A Day at Heathrow

STEWART MACDONALD

Among the many buses and coaches to be seen at London's Heathrow Airport are vehicles like this ex-National Travel (West) Bristol VRL/ECW coach. This one is owned by Margo of Croydon, painted in Thomas Cook livery.

Operation of RTs by London Transport ceased in 1979. The last RT route to serve Heathrow was 140, which was converted to Routemaster operation in the summer of 1978.

An Alder Valley ex-Southdown Leyland Leopard/Duple at Heathrow in 1978. It is seen in the yellow and white Railair livery, on the service linking the Airport with Reading, for railway passengers.

In the varied British Airways bus fleet, an AEC Swift, used for airside transfers. More recent buses with this half-cab layout have been Leyland Nationals, as illustrated on page 26

Arguably the hardest-worked Fords in Britain are those operated by Whyte's of Colnbrook in and around Heathrow. As well as providing free inter-terminal transfers involving fairly arduous stop-start work they are used on airport staff services and, as show here, on services for spectators.

Construction work was still being completed at the central bus station in this December 1977 view of a short Leyland National from the London Country fleet running on Green Line service.

Right: The advert says it all. Leyland B15 prototype (now Titan) with London Transport in Pimlico.

A Bedford SB/Duple from the fleet of Bowers, Chapel-en-le-Frith loads outside Queens Building in May 1978.

The Standardised Seventies

As another decade draws to a close, ALAN MILLAR looks back at the many important changes to affect the bus industry since 1970.

So much has happened to the bus industry over the past decade that it is impossible to do justice to all of the events in the short space available to me; But I can touch on a few of the trends and developments which, in autumn 1978, look like being some of the 1970s' hallmarks. Forgive my ignoring the sweeping developments that the reorganisation of local government caused, but these have been dealt with in earlier *Buses Annuals* and deserve a chapter to themselves.

In terms of hardware, the 1970s must be represented by the Leyland National which was unveiled at the 1970 Commercial Motor Show, and which has gone on to appear in most major fleets throughout the country. It represented a totally new concept in British bus design and operation. It was the first — and, as yet, only — example of the almost unattainable . . . the standard city bus. That meant, of course, that it was loved in concept and reality by some, and loathed by others for the same reasons.

More research and original thinking went into National than any bus which preceded it, and the result was a vehicle capable of better performance, offering higher standards of passenger comfort, and constructed with greater impact resistance than any other bus. It looked nothing like anything else on the road, it sounded nothing like anything else on the road, and it shared few components with anything else on the road. That upset many operators when the first examples became available in 1971/72, for their maintenance systems had all been designed to cope with more conventional vehicles.

Their initial impressions were not helped by the many teething troubles experienced with early models, and by the high fuel consumption of the fixed-head Leyland 510 turbocharged diesel. Prototypes had been tested in many conditions throughout the world, but none had been run in British passenger service, and this was being discovered all too painfully.

The early Nationals were also standardised to a degree of obsession. They came as 10.3m or 11.3m models with one or two doors, left or right-hand drive, and with bus seats only. Customer pressure soon put paid to that idea.

Such problems attracted more than their fair share of attention, not least from the dismal Jimmies of the enthusiast fraternity, but, by 1976 when the phase two version was announced, National had matured into a

very dependable model. Some of its features have been written off as gimmickry, and this was acknowledged by the 1978 appearance of a 10.3m B-series rural model — a sort of National Popular — and the Mark Two version, with Leyland TL11 engine, which was launched at the 1978 International Motor Show is also a simpler beast.

The industry may not be sold completely on single-deck urban buses, but with Nationals having run for practically every British operator and for many overseas concerns, its distinctive outline must be a symbol of the 1970s.

Perhaps it was the standard outline of the National which was an inspiration, but even if it wasn't, the industry has devoted more time in the past decade to creating corporate identities than before. Suddenly, the wrappings of the bus service have become as important as the service itself.

The first PTEs started it in the late 1960s, Tyneside and Greater Glasgow, South Yorkshire, and West Yorkshire PTEs all adopted readily identifiable logotypes and catching liveries within weeks of their formation. But top marks must still go to Greater Manchester Transport which inherited and improved upon the orange and white style of Selnec. Its wavy orange stylised M and deep orange basic colour do

much to underline an image — and, for all I know, the image may only be skin deep — of an efficient system.

GMT's subsidiary fleets have also succumbed to the corporate image, with the four coach fleets of Charterplan, Warburtons, Godfrey Abbot, and Lancashire United being decked out in a 'Starsky and Hutch' boomerang style livery with brown/orange, two-tone blue, blue/green, and red/yellow flashes. The LUT bus fleet has even lost its traditional red and grey to become mainly orange; it may be sacrilege, but at least it is done with quality.

Even London Transport rethought its corporate identity, giving up some of the trappings of its long-running style in favour of varying areas of white relief and white LT roundels. Unfortunately, yellow paint went on to entrance doors of so-equipped buses, as if to invite passengers to walk into them when closed!

National Bus had to give itself a corporate identity, for it entered the 1970s as little more than a holding company for a large group of ostensibly unconnected operators. True, the former Tilling companies had an identity forged by a standard vehicle buying policy, but that was all, and the ex-BET companies didn't even have that. Coaches were first to be done, early in 1972, when, overnight, a National coach network was created by painting NBC's coaches in the now-familiar

white livery.

That was a start, and some felt, and still do, that it ought also to have been the finish of the image plan, but buses needed an identity too, and were given it later the same year. This smacked of all the supression-of-the-individual stuff which surrounded the early Leyland Nationals, as there were only two basic colours — poppy red and leaf green — and these could be applied only in bus or semi-coach style. Horror of horrors, we all said, as the long-loved traditional liveries of East Kent, Southdown, City of Oxford and East Yorkshire bit the dust. We chose to stay silent as the dreadful Ribble, Northern General and other schemes improved in new colours. It was all a great levelling process which could have been done with more imagination, but the deed did need to be done.

Scottish Bus Group was jolted by NBC's ideas, but fought shy of the full horror of the English scheme. When it did take its first corporate plunge — early in 1976 — the effect was superb. The M-type motorway coaches used on its overnight and day services to London were decked out in blue and white with bold SCOTTISH name and St Andrew's Saltire logo. They looked good in Scotland, and stood out impressively against shoals of white fish in Victoria Coach Station.

With the gradualism of inevitability (or is it the inevitability of gradualism?), SBG's buses got the corporate bug two years later, but again not as grimly as those at NBC. The strong local colours were kept, but fleetnames were standardised to incorporate the coaches' logo and were applied to the same parts of buses. This hastened the reduction of styles of colour application, but in some cases it tidied up some less than clean liveries (eg Central SMT double-deckers).

Into the mouths of the big fish, as in decades before, disappeared some of the smaller, independent companies for whom it has all proved too much. This is always a cause for great mourning among enthusiast groups, but at least we treasure the memories of the lost fleets. Among the favourites lost to posterity are MacBrayne, its red/green/cream buses absorbed into Scottish Bus Group fleets; King Alfred of Winchester, its green/cream fleet dipped in poppy red by Hants and Dorset; and the separate green fleets of Green Bus of Rugeley and Harper of Heath Hayes eaten by Midland Red. United Auto took Gillett Brothers, and, in the same area, Tyne & Wear PTE took over Economic's South Shields-Sunderland operations.

In all of these cases, buses taken over were run by their new owners for a time at least. The same happened when the Blue Bus fleet of Tailby &

George of Willington was taken over by Derby Corporation in 1973. That remarkable fleet of well-maintained one-offs would have remained with Derby for a long time had it not been for the spectacular events of the night of 5 January 1976 when the depot and 19 buses in it were destroyed by fire. Very sad for enthusiasts, embarrassingly inconvenient for Derby, but what a way to go!

To this list of lost operators one could well add Barton. True, it still thrives as Britain's largest independent, but the 'real' Barton of the countless weird and eccentric buses was wiped out in 1973/74. Leyland PS1 double-deckers, Barton BTD and BTS rebuilds, Yeates-bodied AEC Reliances and Bedford VALs (some with two doors!), and a wide variety of more conventional contraptions had been part of the Barton aura for so long. No doubt, passengers found them lacking in the finesse of more widely-used specimens, but those of us daft enough flocked to them in droves. Now, their place has been taken by a fine fleet of modern Leyland and Bedford luxury coaches which must be appreciated greatly by the company's customers. But they don't entice me to Nottingham or Chilwell in the same way as their predecessors did.

Hordes were still flocking to London throughout the decade to get their last chance of seeing active RTs in

Left: The first Foden-NC — for Greater Manchester — meets the camera head-on near the Sandbach works of Fodens.

Below left: London Transport's AEC Merlins have ended up on only the intensive Red Arrow routes. MBA 588 wore a brighter livery for a short time.

Scottish Bus Group's strong liveries include Highland's bizarre red and blue style, seen here on Alexander-bodied Albion Lowlander before corporate fleetnames were introduced.

service. One might have thought that their fervour would have diminished as the type's death receded closer and closer to 1980, but still they came... and the RTs go on.

The prolonged existence of the 1947-54 RTs is but a symptom of the lurching passage of London Transport through the decade, with one vehicle crisis following another as modern buses are laid up. LT began the decade still buying standee single-deckers in the shape of some 700-odd AEC Swifts, but late 1970 saw the appearance of the first DMS-type Daimler Fleetlines of which 2,646 were bought by 1978.

Suddenly, the long AEC Merlins of 1967-69 were found to be an outright disaster — mainly because they were long and single-deck, rather than because they were Merlins — and an expensive disposal programme was arranged hastily in 1973-76. Some went overseas, some to home market customers, and others for scrap. They were replaced by Fleetlines and Metropolitan double-deckers which, together with Leyland Nationals, were also to oust many of the shorter Swifts which also fell from grace with a bump. On top of all that, before they had all arrived, the Fleetlines were also considered *'busa non grata'*, and few are expected to last long into the 1980s.

LT has found itself, through all of its tortuous bus buying policies, in the front line of the latest stage of the double-deck bus war, with MCW Metrobuses and Leyland Titans competing to become LT bus of the 1980s.

It's been quite a decade for double-deck bus development, with several manufacturers springing into the market with alternatives to what had become a British Leyland staple diet. MCW started with the Scania-based Metropolitan, while Ailsa Bus took the

bit very much between its teeth with the front-engined Volvo Ailsa. Northern Counties, fearing losses of orders to builders of integral buses, persuaded Fodens to build the Gardner-engined Foden-NC, but it looks like dying out with only eight built at the time of writing.

Next on the scene was Hestair Dennis, the revitalised Guildford builder of fire engines, dustcarts, and buses of old, which developed its Dominator as a no-nonsense souped-up Fleetline. With it, for export markets, was launched the Jubilant front-engined bus, a vehicle which shamed Leyland into selling the Leyland (formerly Guy) Victory as an export 'decker.

The double-decker has also been challenged by a continental creation — the articulated single-decker. South Yorkshire PTE began to test vehicles in 1977, the first to be tried being a joint British-Danish-Swiss machine, a Leyland-DAB with Saurer engine. A Swedish Volvo B58 came early in 1978 and was followed by another later the same year, while German builder MAN sent over the first right-hand drive model — Bendibus — soon after. How few or many artic buses run in this country no one can tell, but MAN's catchy model name has become imprinted quickly on the public's mind as an apt term for any artic.

Of course, much more has happened over the past decade, but the 1980s will have to be good if they are even to contain the delights which I have mentioned in these few pages.

Overleaf: Two ads for sadly-missed Harrington coach bodies. The Cavalier ad dates from 1961, and that for the short-lived Legionnaire from 1964.

the
Harrington
CAVALIER

The Cavalier is an entirely new luxury coach body, suitable for all under-floor engined chassis. Wrap-round windscreens and rear glasses, luxury seating for 41 passengers, improved passenger visibility and roof ventilation are outstanding features of this new design.

 # Thomas Harrington Ltd.

SACKVILLE WORKS, HOVE, SUSSEX, ENGLAND.
TELEGRAMS: VEHICLES, BRIGHTON, TELEPHONE: HOVE 37555-6-7.

SPECIALISTS IN COACHWORK FOR OVER SIXTY YEARS